VOLUME 91 • NUMBER 3 • FALL 2002

NATIONAL

CIVIC

REVIEW

MAKING CITIZEN DEMOCRACY WORK

IN THIS ISSUE

Social Capital and New Urbanist Design

Christopher T. Gates

President, National Civic League

Robert Loper

Editor

A Publication of the National Civic League and Jossey-Bass

NATIONAL CIVIC REVIEW (ISSN 0027-9013) is published quarterly by Wiley Subscription Services, Inc., A Wiley Company, at Jossey-Bass, 989 Market Street, San Francisco, CA 94103-1741, and the National Civic League, 1445 Market Street, Suite 300, Denver, CO 80202-1717. NCL, founded in 1894 as the National Municipal League, advocates a new civic agenda to create communities that work for everyone. NCL is a 501(c)(3) nonprofit, nonpartisan educational association of individuals and organizations. NCL members have access to the information and services necessary to improve community life. For complete information, contact Derek Okubo, (303) 571-4343.

INDEXED in Public Affairs Information Service, ABC POL SCI, and Book Review Index.

SUBSCRIPTIONS for individuals are $60 per year in the United States, Canada, and Mexico, and $84 per year in the rest of the world. Subscriptions for institutions are $115 in the United States, $155 in Canada and Mexico, and $189 in the rest of the world. To order subscriptions, single issues, or reprints, please refer to the Ordering Information page at the back of this issue.

PERIODICALS postage paid at San Francisco, California, and at additional mailing offices. POSTMASTER: send address changes to National Civic Review, Jossey-Bass Inc., 989 Market Street, San Francisco, CA 94103-1741.

NCL MEMBERS send change of address to Debbie Gettings, National Civic League, 1445 Market Street, Suite 300, Denver, CO 80202-1717.

EDITORIAL CORRESPONDENCE should be sent to Robert Loper, National Civic League, 1319 F Street NW, Suite 204, Washington, DC 20004.

www.josseybass.com

LETTERS TO THE EDITOR. *National Civic Review* welcomes letters to the editor. Write to *National Civic Review*, 1319 F Street, Suite 204, Washington, DC 20004, or send e-mail to robert@ncldc.org. Please include your name, address, and telephone number.

CONTENTS

NOTE FROM THE PRESIDENT

The nineteenth-century German philosopher Arthur Schopenhauer suggested that all truths pass through three stages: first they are ridiculed, then they are violently opposed, and finally they are accepted as self-evident. Though somewhat anachronistic, this observation usefully reminds us of the passions that may accompany debate over new public ideas. As our response to the terrorist attacks enters its second year and the prospect of invading Iraq grows, the claim that New Urbanist design principles can enhance formation of social capital may not resonate strongly enough to win a prominent place on the public agenda. But the challenges we face in our society, and the choices that we must make, give us good reason to take an interest in policies and practices that might help to increase the bonds of trust and reciprocity among us.

We are still finding our way in a much-changed world. It has scarcely been a generation since the economic shocks of the 1973 oil crisis set in motion a sequence of events that would lead to the end of big-government liberalism. Today's political economy of reinvented government and deregulated markets faces the twin challenges of corporate governance and an unprecedented threat to the nation's security. We have seen a wild ride in the stock market that first created and then erased trillions of dollars in value. Although as the world's sole superpower our influence on global affairs has never been greater, we are clearly not free from harm. We have learned that complacency is not an option and that we must reinvigorate our collective engagement in the arts of self-government.

As we consider the public agenda in these uncertain times, there is no shortage of concerns that command our attention. For this issue of the *National Civic Review,* we at NCL have chosen to focus on the potential impact of New Urbanist design principles on the creation of social capital. Since the publication of Robert Putnam's book *Bowling Alone,* there has been a lively public debate over social capital: what constitutes it, how it can be measured, whether it is changing, and what if anything can be done to increase the level of trust and rejuvenate the reciprocal ties among us. The underlying ethos of New Urbanism rests on the premise that how we design our communities affects how we live our lives. Communities that are denser, less car-dependent, and have a diverse mix of residential, business, and retail elements (it is argued) promote more interaction among their residents, leading to an increase in bonding social capital in particular.

That our country can engage in this debate over how we should live even as our way of life has been violently attacked does us credit. As the articles in this issue indicate, more research is needed to evaluate whether and how social capital is created in New Urbanist communities.

The article by Thomas Sander should become the essential starting point for anyone interested in this topic. He gives us a comprehensive introduction to the issues, assesses what has been learned so far, and indicates directions for further research.

Bruce Podobnik presents results from comparative analysis of neighborhoods in Portland, Oregon, that suggest a high level of bonding social capital in the New Urbanist development. But, as he notes, self-selection by the residents in choosing to move into the community created a homogeneous neighborhood that one would expect to have a high level of bonding social capital. As the composition of the community shifts over the years, it would be instructive to track any changes in either bonding or bridging social capital.

Thad Williamson's article on sprawl and political participation presents a methodologically sophisticated analysis of the effects of community characteristics on measures of civic engagement. This research is ongoing, but one thing that Williamson shows is that reduced dependence on the automobile is a strong predictor of political participation.

Williamson's analysis complements the concerns Rick Porth raises in his discussion of the regional challenges besetting central cities and suburbs and the policies needed to address them. It is clear that how we formulate urban policy and foster suburban expansion has to be changed. We cannot continue to think that we are only the next subdivision away from the American dream. Progress in dealing with these issues requires collaboration among a diverse set of interests.

John McKoy's account of the civic lessons learned through multisectoral collaboration highlights the importance of civic intermediary organizations in convening discussion and fostering productive relationships among a range of actors.

Whatever eventual impact New Urbanism has on social capital, redesigning our communities to make them less automobile-centric can have a number of positive effects, especially given the political risks attendant to our dependence on imported oil and the concern over the relationship of carbon dioxide emissions to global warming. Although it is clear that moving to a New Urbanist community does not solve any of our problems, part of the responsibility inherent in self-government is the obligation to become more attentive to the collective impact of our daily choices. Knowledge of this kind is an essential element in creating political wisdom—a commodity that, like social capital, we cannot have too much of.

CHRISTOPHER T. GATES
PRESIDENT, NATIONAL CIVIC LEAGUE

Social Capital and New Urbanism: Leading a Civic Horse to Water?

Thomas H. Sander

New Urbanism has been ascendant in the last several decades, riding its promise as a strategy to reduce suburban sprawl and automobile dependence, while increasingly fostering stronger communities. The number of neighborhood-scale New Urbanist projects completed or under way rose 37 percent in 2001 to more than two hundred developments in thirty-nine states, up from a 25 percent increase in 1999 and a 28 percent increase in 2000.[1]

But does New Urbanism work? Does New Urbanist design produce stronger communities, viewed through the lens of social capital? This is not an easy research task, so in this article I discuss research challenges as well as possible approaches. Given the complexity of this issue, it is perhaps best to start with a review of social capital and New Urbanism before considering their interaction.[2]

Social Capital

Most of us have a general sense of how our social ties matter to us personally. Some hyperactive "networkers" in the 1980s or 1990s exhibit a more wholesale embrace of the importance of social connections. The folk wisdom that more people get their jobs from *whom* they know rather than *what* they know turns out to be true.[3]

A burgeoning literature[4] over the last decade shows that social capital[5]—social networks and the attendant norms of trust and reciprocity—is central to many of the collective goods we care about, among them safe streets, healthy and happy citizens, effective education, responsive democracy, and children's welfare. Thus social ties help us not only *personally* but also *collectively*.[6]

There remains much to understand about social capital, but it is clear that with a base of trust we can engage in reciprocal behavior, doing things for others without any immediate or direct expectation of repayment, with confidence that we (or others in our group) will ultimately benefit. We tend to develop reciprocity with specific individuals whom we know (friends, family, work colleagues, members of a common group) as well as with larger groups (our workplace, neighborhood, church) and the community at large. This latter generalized reciprocity is especially valuable to communities since, as Robert Putnam has written, it lubricates social interaction in the same way cash is more efficient than barter. You can undertake an action without having to separately negotiate the terms of each exchange.[7]

How does a social network strengthen norms of trust and reciprocity? First, a social network makes it easier for a community to learn who is and is not trustworthy. This increases the cost of being untrustworthy since one might incur a communitywide loss in reputation for the individual gains to be had from being untrustworthy with one community member. In addition, since social capital tends to flow in virtuous circles, each positive collaboration helps inspire and pattern future cooperation.

How do social networks, trust, and reciprocity enhance community well-being? First, they facilitate mobilizing others (whether for a social movement or simply to help a neighbor-in-need). Second, they improve information flow, helping us learn of anything from a job lead to a potential partner or community news or who can be trusted. Third, the existence of trust avoids the necessity of a third-party mechanism (such as government or a lawyer) to reinforce prosocial cooperative behavior. Fourth, in a trusting community, residents engage less in unproductive defensive behavior—watching their back, writing a "defensive memo" at work, locking their doors, and so on.

New Urbanism

New Urbanism[8] is neither new nor focused just on traditionally urban areas. Building on the Garden City and City Beautiful movements and harking back to livable towns (Charleston, Savannah), New Urbanists believe that "urbanism" can work in a community of any scale and is as appropriate in a new growth area or suburb as in the central city. By *urbanism*, they mean a community that is:

- Diverse (mixed residential, business, and retail developments; and ideally mixed demographics, facilitated, for example, by putting a modest apartment over a garage or above a ground-floor shop)
- Walkable (shops ideally within a five-minute walk of home, walking paths, and streets laid out on a grid pattern, with no cul-de-sacs[9])
- Not automobile-centric (garage hidden in a back alley, parallel parking rather than in a lot)
- Not gated
- Marked by a clear center and edges

Such a community has accessible and useful public space, has safe and inviting streets (they are narrow and houses have front porches and windows that face the street), and is linked to public transportation.

The New Urbanism came to prominence in 1981 when DPZ (the design firm of Andres Duany and his wife, Elizabeth Plater-Zyberk) built the resort town of Seaside on the Florida panhandle.

When interest in such developments started to mount, seven prominent New Urbanists (architects Peter Calthorpe, Duany, Plater-Zyberk, Elizabeth Moule, Stefanos Polyzoides, and Daniel Solomon, as well as organizer Peter Katz) founded the Congress for the New Urbanism (CNU) to promote and disseminate information about New Urbanism. They held their first congress in 1993, at which 170 designers compared works-in-progress and exchanged ideas about urban and suburban places.

New Urbanists codified central elements of their movement in the CNU charter, developed from 1993 to 1996 and ratified in 1996. The charter articulates design principles at various levels (region, town, street, and so on). Despite the charter, New Urbanism remains somewhat murky at the edges. CNU tries to solidify the core of this movement by issuing awards; showcasing new developments; and networking developers, policy makers, architects, and others. But there is no New Urbanist certification for a site (despite a list kept by *New Urban News*) and some sites claim to be New Urbanist that probably aren't.[10]

The early sites tended to be exclusively "greenfield" developments (on undeveloped suburban or rural land). The vast majority are still greenfield, but there has been an increase in "grayfield" developments (as in converting a mall or industrial plant tract into a New Urbanist development) and "infill" projects (for instance, redesigning and densifying a suburban traffic corridor along New Urbanist principles). In addition, efforts to convert run-down and problem-plagued high-rise public housing into lower-density, mixed-income use have recently (under HOPE VI) been modeled on New Urbanist principles.[11]

What Might Be the Connection of New Urbanism to Social Capital?

The idea that our built environment can importantly shape the quality of our democracy, our lives, and the well-working of our communities has a long lineage.

In the late 1800s, Progressive Era reformers explicitly invented playgrounds to afford a space for socially disconnected urban immigrant youth.[12] Progressive Era leaders also advanced the City Beautiful movement, advocating that beautiful cities could eliminate social ills, inspire moral rectitude among the poor, and attract the upper class to work and spend money in urban areas.

After World War I, the Garden City movement picked up steam in Great Britain and in the United States (as in Radburn, New Jersey),[13] attempting to foster higher quality of life and greater civic connection through clustered housing knit together, with schools and public facilities, by greenways and walkways. They aimed to exploit the best of city and country.

In the 1960s, various North Americans focused on the connection between urban design and civic engagement. In 1961, Jane Jacobs published *The Death and Life of Great American Cities,* criticizing contemporary urban planning for ignoring design that enabled residents to reduce crime by having "eyes on the street." Her theories were revived by New Urbanists, who lauded the idea of the front porch. Another American, William Whyte, assisting the New York City Planning Commission in 1969, conducted his Street Life Project, demonstrating through time-lapse photography that small public spaces improve urban civic and social life.

This whirlwind tour makes it evident that claiming the built environment can improve civic life is hardly original with the New Urbanists. Nevertheless, some New Urbanist ideas seem especially promising today. For example, given the increased segregation of our communities and the difficulty of building cross-race and cross-class social ties,[14] the HOPE VI mixed-income developments may offer newfound hope. Duany, defending the mandated uniformity of housing styles within HOPE VI sites, commented that you need a "shared syntax of architecture" (similar housing exteriors) to make diverse people comfortable in living cheek-to-jowl.[15] But the interesting question is whether the housing uniformity and physical proximity of diverse populations in a HOPE VI development actually leads to greater cross-race and cross-class social bonds.[16]

What Are the Challenges in Seeing Whether It Works?

There are four central challenges to evaluating whether New Urbanism leads to more social capital: (1) the influence of the outside world, (2) the projects' infancy, (3) selection bias, and (4) the Hawthorne effect.

First, New Urbanist developments and theory don't operate in a vacuum; they must take root in the real world. For example, New Urbanists strive to create a mixed-use development wherein residents live, shop, and work locally. But do they? Many New Urbanist town residents don't have employment locally and need to commute. Local developments generally contain retail shops, but rarely are they on the scale of a Wal-Mart, Costco, or Home Depot.[17] There are anecdotal stories of New Urbanist residents getting milk and eggs locally, or patronizing local stores to some extent, but still using a megastore for better prices or a more distant mall to find greater retail store variety. Reports of Celebration, Florida, indicate that the downtown caters more to tourists than residents.[18] Residents can also subvert designers' intent; some Seaside, Florida, residents built a rear porch (rather than use the front porch provided) or let their hedge grow far higher to increase privacy.[19] This is why New Urbanism may only be leading a civic horse to water.

Second, it is extremely early in the game. Many New Urbanist developments are not even fully built. Will the towns' character change as the scale increases? If these towns have an especially civic culture, will that survive as owners sell to new residents? Research today is important, but it can be likened to declaring the winner or loser of a ballgame in the first inning. History shows how early prognostication can be wrong. For example, Levittown and other early post–World War II suburbs were criticized as sterile,[20] but Herbert Gans[21] showed just how civic Levittown was. Some "new communities" built in the 1960s and 1970s, such as Columbia, Maryland, and Reston, Virginia, were also heavily criticized initially even though they now seem relatively successful in civic terms.[22] Some residents' early enthusiasm with Celebration quickly soured around disputes with the developer over the character of a new school.[23]

Third is selection bias. New Urbanist developments market themselves as community-friendly towns. Thus, if a New Urbanist development is unusually civic, it may be more of a *marketing* success (in attracting community-minded residents) than an indication of how the town's *design* influenced the residents.[24] The civic engagement of residents of Reston certainly had as much to do with marketing it to potential buyers as a place of engagement and fostering a civic culture as to any specific design element.[25] Residents of (basically New Urbanist) Harbor Town, Tennessee, believed that their high level of social interaction was accounted for by an unusually social mix of residents.[26]

Without randomized experiments of the sort that are rare in social science,[27] the best that researchers can do is to compare the social capital of residents at a New Urbanist site against the historic level of civic engagement at their prior, non-New Urbanist residence.[28] Methodologically, unless there is a waiting list, one cannot know who will move to the New Urbanist community and thus cannot collect information about civic behavior and attitude *before* the person moves. Relying on people's memory of their civic engagement in their prior community once they've moved often leads to distortion of the past (since residents may want to believe they are more engaged now).

In addition to a higher civic mix of residents making the *average* New Urbanist town resident look more civic, the *concentration* of civic-minded residents also enhances the town's social capital. To understand why, imagine the difficulty of mobilizing others if you were a rare social creature in a community. Much as species collapse without a critical population base, civic engagement requires a certain core level of interest, and given its appeal to civic-minded residents a New Urbanist community is more likely to possess it. Thus, even comparing residents' current and prior levels of social capital does not isolate the design impact of the New Urbanist community, since the residents surely find it easier to galvanize others into social activities.

Fourth is the Hawthorne effect. Participants in an experiment want so much to show that interventions work that they change their behavior to make them work.[29] This is similar to the placebo effect, where participants in a medical experiment who are taking a sugar pill with no medicinal effect (but thinking they are taking a pill that has valuable medical impact) show improvement over their baseline condition simply from the power of their positive thinking. Thus, especially in the early years of a New Urbanist community, it is hard to separate out genuine New Urbanist results from residents either wanting to make the experiment succeed or feeling as though they are taking a powerful civic pill.

Armed with this understanding of the difficulties of proving the case, we can now review what data exist on the impact of New Urbanism on social capital.

Does It Work?

First, I consider general research concerning the impact of demographic heterogeneity, commuting time, and population density on civic engagement—a synecdoche of social capital that focuses not only on social networks and trust but also on associated behavior such as political engagement or volunteering.[30]

New Urbanist developments (through a variety of housing types within each development) aspire to promote greater income and ethnic diversity than in a standard development. Assuming New Urbanists succeed in achieving greater heterogeneity (and there are significant caveats[31]), what is the likely impact on civic engagement? David Campbell has integrated his own interesting analytical research with a rapidly growing body of literature and concluded that diversity increases *political* participation (influencing public policy, motivated largely by self-interest) while decreasing *civic* participation (other forms of civic engagement, social networks, and trust that are motivated largely by norms of reciprocity and social expectations).[32] This suggests that if the New Urbanist community is more diverse, it has a harder time *ceteris paribus* building civic engagement, social networks, and trust.

One hopeful piece of evidence for the New Urbanism comes from Putnam's analysis showing how a longer commute reduces civic engagement. Putnam found that

> the car and the commute . . . are demonstrably bad for community life. In round numbers the evidence suggests that *each additional ten minutes in daily commuting time cuts involvement in community affairs by 10 percent*— fewer public meetings attended, fewer committees chaired, fewer petitions signed, fewer church services attended, less volunteering, and so on. In fact, although commuting time is not quite as powerful an influence on civic involvement as education, it is more important than almost any other demographic factor. And time diary studies suggest that there is a similarly

strong negative effect of commuting time on informal social interaction. [emphasis in original[33]]

That New Urbanist communities aim to reduce commuting time by combining residence and business, and try to reduce dependence on automobiles through creating a more walkable community, could bolster civic engagement.

Political scientist Thad Williamson also found a negative civic impact from sprawl, although he is less sanguine about the opportunity for boosting civic engagement through reducing sprawl (see his article in this issue of the *National Civic Review*). Analyzing the 2000 Social Capital Community Benchmark Survey,[34] he found that a longer commuting time depresses local-level social trust, and that communities with a high percentage of solo commuters have lower participation in various civic and social activities. Williamson also found that living in the central city positively predicts both an individual's level of political interest and most forms of political participation (especially voting, attending marches, and membership in political or reform organizations). Central city residence, however, was *not* associated with greater attendance at public meetings, active involvement with more voluntary groups, a higher level of social trust, or decreased alienation.[35]

But Williamson differs with Putnam in that, as laudable as he finds the goal of reducing auto dependence or commuting time, he concludes that we are unlikely to reduce average commute time enough to significantly increase America's stock of social capital.[36]

What About Research on the New Urbanism Specifically?

New Urbanism seems a domain with more "success stories" than verifiable successes. However, despite the paucity of evidence, what is known?

First there are studies of new construction. One of the most rigorous and thoughtful evaluations of New Urbanism comes from Barbara Brown and Vivian Cropper, who compared a New Urbanist subdivision ten miles from Salt Lake City, Utah, with a neighboring standard suburban subdivision.[37] The New Urbanist community, in which eighty-one units were built, had accessory apartments over back alley garages that increased density and diversity, small lot sizes, front porches, shallow setbacks, and narrower streets. The town was marketed for its amenities, not as a New Urbanist community, and was thus less prone to attracting especially civic residents. Although the commercial center, the high-density town homes, and the light rail stop had yet to be built,[38] there was within walking distance a community center, a swimming pool, a golf course, and pedestrian paths.

The standard subdivision had 127 houses of similar price and square footage (although on larger lots without accessory apartments) to those in the

New Urbanist community, prominent garages, small entry landings rather than front porches, wider streets, sidewalks, cul-de-sacs, and no commercial area.

Brown and Cropper achieved an impressive 65–67 percent response rate among homeowners (partly by offering a small financial incentive to complete the survey) but were not able to survey accessory apartment renters.

The Utah New Urbanist residents demonstrated a statistically significant higher rate of neighborliness (knowing neighbors, borrowing from neighbors, visiting, speaking and socializing with neighbors, watching neighbors' homes, and expressing willingness to improve the neighborhood), but no statistically significant higher sense of community (measured on a twelve-item scale measuring self-reported feelings of membership, perceived ability to influence the nature of the neighborhood, shared emotional connections, and needs fulfillment) than their standard suburban counterparts.[39] The survey controlled for difference in length of residency between the New Urbanist and standard suburbs and for the level of preexisting ties in the neighborhood.[40] The only cautions on the survey are, first, that there still may have been some selection effects both among the New Urbanist residents (that is, the design may have attracted civic-minded residents even if the site was not expressly marketed that way) and the standard suburban residents (those seeking more privacy). Both of these could exaggerate the design impact of New Urbanism. Second, the survey did not control for any differences between the suburban and New Urban communities, other than tenure in community and preexisting ties.[41]

Joongsub Kim compared Kentlands (an acclaimed New Urbanist development near Gaithersburg, Maryland) to Orchard Village (a neighboring standard subdivision).[42] Kentlands was two-thirds occupied at the time of research and had completed a retail (mall-like) development but not its downtown retail center. Kim's survey found a statistically significant higher level of a chance encounter with a resident from another section of the community and higher participation in community activities.[43] But Kim found no statistically significant evidence that Kentlands' residents interacted more with next-door neighbors or cared more for other residents—the other two types of social interaction measured.[44]

The plus of Kim's study is that he employed Orchard Village as a comparison (although he did not control for any demographic differences); the minus is that his results were likely confounded by selection effects (that is, Kentlands marketing attracted more social and civic residents and Orchard Village probably attracted a far less civic mix) and concentration effects (it was easier to socialize with others since the random Kentlands resident was more social).

Bruce Podobnik, of Lewis and Clark College, compared a Portland New Urbanist development, Orenco Station, against an established neighborhood in northeast Portland.[45] Orenco Station is in the affluent, high-tech, western region of Portland metropolitan area known as Oregon's "Silicon Forest." The residents began occupying the site in summer 2001. It contained a town center with a coffee shop, grocery store, numerous restaurants, other retail establishments, a central park and a clubhouse with pool; other portions of the site were under construction. Like most New Urbanist sites, the development was pedestrian-friendly and had small lot sizes, high density, and common spaces and parks. Orenco Station residents were more likely (59 percent) than northeast Portland residents (45 percent) to report that their community was friendlier than their prior residence was. Seventy-eight percent of those in Orenco Station reported a greater sense of community than in their prior neighborhood, compared to 46 percent in northeast Portland who felt this way. Finally, 40 percent of households participated in formal or informal groups, versus 30 percent in northeast Portland.

However, there are some methodological concerns about this study. First, there are substantial questions about whether northeast Portland is an appropriate comparison.[46] Second, there are likely to be significant selection effects from the Orenco Station residents since the marketing and design catered to civic-minded residents. For example, only one resident of Orenco Station complained of a lack of privacy despite the site's high density. Third, the face-to-face interviews may lead respondents to be less candid, but given that this interviewing approach was employed in both Orenco Station and northeast Portland, it shouldn't explain differences between the two communities.

"Insights from the Front Porch" reports on Harbor Town, a largely New Urbanist community neighboring downtown Memphis, Tennessee.[47] Researchers mapped the social networks of twenty-one Harbor Town respondents and concluded that people who lived on publicly used spaces (such as a square, or a riverfront park that attracted residents from throughout the community) tended to have far more geographically dispersed friendships than people who lived away from such a site. The report also suggested—consistent with the experience of Andrew Ross, who lived in Celebration, Florida, for a year—that the lack of privacy in New Urbanist design may force residents to be congenial with most residents and simultaneously encourage them to save their closest friendships for those living further away.[48]

Harbor Town was also compared with Riverwood Farms,[49] a conventional suburb of similar vintage located thirty minutes from Memphis. Slightly over a quarter of Riverwood residents reported a lack of neighborhood feeling (26 percent) versus fewer than 5 percent of Harbor Town respondents. One quarter of Riverwood respondents felt "isolated from others in their community," significantly higher than the 15 percent who felt isolated in Harbor Town. Harbor Town residents had larger social networks among neighbors, even though residents of both neighborhoods had a similar number of close neighbor friends and neighbors they visited with regularly.[50]

The plus of this study was the existence of the Riverwood comparison group, but the minus is that there may have been significant selection effects in that Harbor Town attracted especially civic-minded residents and Riverwood likely attracted people who were much less so inclined. The 21 percent response rates were relatively low, and the study did not examine or control for demographic differences between Harbor Town and Riverwood respondents. The Harbor Town study, in its focus on "neighborhood" networks and friends, also did not examine whether Riverwood residents made up for their smaller neighborhood social networks by having more social friends outside the neighborhood than in Harbor Town.

In Florida, a mail-in survey[51] conducted by the twelve-year-old son of husband-wife authors of a book on Celebration revealed that 72 percent of Celebration reported knowing more neighbors there than in their previous residence, a third said they knew everyone on the street, and two-thirds said they knew some people on their street. Approximately 70 percent participated in block parties, one quarter participated in the PTA, and 60 percent attended community meetings. These numbers are high compared to nationwide averages, but (1) the survey did not control for the demographics of Celebration, (2) the methodology of the survey is not provided so one does not know if only the most civic slice of Celebration was reached, (3) there is no group against which Celebration is compared, and (4) the question asking how many neighbors are known relies on respondents' (unreliable) memory.

Finally, in a different vein, Keith Hampton at MIT did a lost-letter experiment in which researchers dispersed sixty lost letters in each of seventy-one urban communities and measured the percentage of letters returned unopened.[52] (Lost-letter results tend to track with levels of communitywide social capital since they reflect residents' willingness to expend energy to benefit an anonymous "other.") There were only two New Urbanist communities in the sample (Celebration and Seaside), but Celebration led the entire survey with 86 percent of letters returned. Seaside's performance was 65.4 percent, slightly above the average, among the seventy-one communities, of 59.4 percent. Although Hampton has not yet published results controlling responses for the town's demographics, early analysis leads him to expect that the performance of Seaside and Celebration on average, controlling for their demographics, was on par with a standard middle-class suburb.[53]

HOPE VI

Leslie Pollner studied the two HOPE VI developments in the Roxbury community in Boston, Mission Main and Orchard Gardens. Orchard Gardens is 43 percent African American, 39 percent Hispanic, and 18 percent other. Mission Main is 46 percent African American, 26 percent Hispanic, and 28 percent other. The Boston sites are at the high end of HOPE VI nationwide in the percentage of public housing residents (83 percent at Mission Main, and 85 percent at Orchard Gardens).[54] Pollner found an unimpressive level of bridging social capital at the Boston sites: "The delimited interaction reported by residents . . . as evidenced by the fact that community involvement rarely exceeds neighborly pleasantries and favors . . . reflects a lack of 'investment' in and identification with their HOPE VI development as a community. In particular, there appear to be two communities co-existing at each site with 'old'[55] residents viewing the development as a 'home' and newer residents viewing the development as a 'stepping stone' to more permanent accommodations."[56] Moreover, not one resident interviewed at the Boston HOPE VI sites had learned of a job from another resident, partly because of the relative absence of bridging social ties.[57]

Looking at social capital more generally, Pollner found relatively frequent favors performed for each other, or in some cases neighbors checking on each other, but almost all respondents reported that it is hard to get to know neighbors and that there is a low sense of community engagement. The tenant task force at Mission Main, whose members wanted to plan social activities, was saddled with financial issues. The Orchard Gardens task force was preoccupied with a new school opening in 2003. Some residents reported not getting involved in their community from a misimpression that participating in community organizing or tattling on neighbors could jeopardize their residency at the development.[58] Pollner's analysis underscores the complexity of designing an environment to foster bridging social capital, and it buttresses Marshall Gans's position that "neighbors are found, but friends are chosen, and class, race, and life stage, not proximity, appear to be the key factors in this process."[59]

Art Naparstek, in *HOPE VI: Community Building Makes A Difference,*[60] describes interesting and exemplary community building activities occurring at seven HOPE VI sites. But his design—looking at the best examples and not controlling for the dramatic demographic changes before and after HOPE VI, a focus only on the assets in each community, and so forth—makes it hard to sort out both how representative the seven cases are of HOPE VI in general or of their communities. Second, if a community did change from HOPE VI, the approach makes it hard to assess how much resulted from a change in inhabitants rather than the physical design of the communities.

Retrofitting Existing Developments

Although it is not common, sites redesigned along New Urbanist principles may be interesting for analysis, since they minimize selection effects by having a relatively constant population before and after the renovation.

Diggs Town, a barracks-style public housing project in Norfolk, Virginia, is such an example.[61] The site was riddled with drug dealers, trash-strewn spaces, and crime, primarily because units lacked any private outdoor space, common space was often not publicly visible, there were large "no man's land" areas that no one took ownership of, and the site was inaccessible to automobile traffic. In the 1990s, Diggs Town was redesigned along New Urbanist lines: front porches were added (to provide eyes on the street), units were given individual addresses and private front and rear yard space with a picket fence delimiting boundaries, the "superblocks" were broken into smaller units, and the streets were relaid to facilitate auto traffic.

The changes resulted in significant anecdotal improvement. Police calls dropped from twenty-five to thirty per day to two to three per week. Yards were much better kept up and commonly were planted and cared for by the individual owners. However, the authors note that one of the challenges of assessing the physical redesign of Diggs Town alone is that "Diggs Town's revitalization came packaged with a host of social interventions."[62]

The Washington Elms (Cambridge, Massachusetts) public housing is another such site.[63] Approximately two hundred units in three-story garden-type buildings were renovated in the 1980s so that units had a private entry rather than a common corridor, and multiple units shared a common rear space, entered only from the individual units' rear door. Washington Elms experienced a significant drop in crime in the ensuing years. Interestingly, however, although the management of Washington Elms ascribed the drop in crime to the redesign, a paper by Laura Siegel (albeit based on an extremely small random sample of four residents) found that residents felt the design changes led to *less* social capital, and that the drop in crime was unrelated to the design changes.[64] Residents said it was now harder to know neighbors, the new semi-private backyards were rarely used, and they lamented the loss of common benches and truly common space.[65]

Conclusions and Implications for Future Research

The evidence to date about the civic impact of New Urbanism is not yet compelling, although the Brown and Kim studies come close to showing that the design may have some effect on neighborliness. Researchers should look for an opportunity to better bolster New Urbanist claims. There are some questions worth probing and three distinct categories worth analyzing further: the rehabbing of existing sites, HOPE VI projects, and New Urbanist developments in general.

Questions Asked. The studies tend to ask about "sense of community," neighborhood behavior, or neighborhood social networks. Studies could benefit from a broader list of social capital questions: asking about the degree of bridging relationships (those crossing lines of race or class), so-called "radius of trust" questions (asking about the degree of trust with others in various circles: "your neighborhood, your town, your workplace," and so on), political engagement, volunteering and philanthropy, involvement in voluntary groups, and so on. A list of these questions can be found in the Social Capital Community Benchmark Survey we conducted in 2000.[66] A broad list would help researchers understand such questions as whether social networks lead to a higher level of trust; whether informal socializing translates into political engagement, volunteering, or civic engagement; whether the social networks are primarily with bonded "like individuals" or bridged with others across race or class; and whether stronger neighborhood social networks are at the expense of social networks outside the neighborhood.

What Are Some Promising Design Methodologies? The foregoing analysis suggests some areas for future research to advance our understanding of the relations between New Urbanist communities and social capital.

Rehabbing of Existing Sites. Researchers should search for more examples on the order of Diggs Town and Washington Elms. Though they may be rare, they are an optimal research site since the population stays relatively constant before and after the rehabbing, and thus it is far easier to isolate the impact of the design change on civic attitudes and behaviors through careful before-and-after measurement. However, at least in their early years these projects still have to deal with the Hawthorne and placebo effects outlined earlier.

HOPE VI Projects. The HOPE VI program is an important stream of New Urbanism, given America's increased residential segregation, and the difficulty of developing bridging social ties across major cleavage such as race or class. Pollner's analysis of the Boston Mission Main and Orchard Gardens projects is discouraging in its suggestion that these sites have not built much bridging social capital. The question is whether the Boston experience is the norm or the exception. It seems plausible, given the variation of design from one HOPE VI site to another, that results at other sites might differ. Here are a few areas (and some possible questions) that might make the experience at other sites different from Boston's:

- *Places for shared interaction.* Do market units and subsidized units share common walkways? Do these units exit on different sides of a building or the same? Are there other common spaces to foster mingling?[67] Are there settings (gymnasium, day care facility, school, community center) for the entire HOPE VI unit that could foster bridging relationships?[68]
- *Floating units.* Some HOPE VI sites have specific units in the complex that are always for subsidized residents, and others commit to an overall ratio of subsidized and market-rate but "float" which units are subsidized or market-rate every time a unit turns over.
- *Demographic mix of residents.* How does the long-term commitment of Mission Main or Orchard Park residents compare with that at other sites, and what is the frequency of turnover?[69] How long have the residents lived there?[70] Does Boston's heavier weighting toward economically poor residents affect the social interaction at the site?
- *Residents' councils.* An interesting potential proxy for the level of bridging social capital at these HOPE VI sites may be whether there is one housing association for the whole development, or a housing association for public housing residents and another for market-rate units. The residents are legally entitled under HUD regulations to a separate housing association (although there has been some talk of potentially changing this), and some of the variation site to site may have much to do with the attitudes of the housing authority managers at the local sites.[71] Nevertheless, sites that have a well-working residents' association for *all* residents may either have an easier time

building bridging social capital or evince the site's commitment to working together.

• *Social organizing.* Is there any entity that receives funding to plan social activities for the whole housing complex? Are the Boston results on lower bridging social capital and community engagement the result of the tenant task forces at Boston's two HOPE VI sites having to focus on nonsocial issues (such as financial issues or the opening of a school)?

For the Bulk of New Urbanist Developments. Most sites are not rehab and are not HOPE VI. They run into all the same design problems suggested earlier (selection bias among both the New Urban residents and the standard suburban residents, sites early in their development, concentration effects, and so on). Two lines of research may be helpful in trying to overcome these design problems.

First, New Urbanist sites may retain a waiting list of people interested in a unit when one becomes available (or at least individuals who have toured the site). These individuals may be a good research pool since they may have a civic disposition similar to that of current or ultimate residents but are probably not currently living in a New Urbanist community. Researchers could compare the civic attitudes and behaviors of people on the list to those in the New Urbanist development, standardizing for demographic differences (income, race, marital status, years lived in the community, and so on). Another approach would be to gather baseline civic measurements of those on the list and then follow up with individuals who move into a New Urbanist development to see how their behavior differs three to five years after they buy a unit.[72]

Second, the Utah and Kentlands analyses are interesting, but the former is not regarded as an exemplary New Urbanist community and the latter clearly attracted an especially civic lot. As the number of New Urban communities increases, researchers should look for a highly regarded New Urbanist community that does not expressly market itself as "community-oriented" and conduct some of the same controlled analyses that Brown and Cropper, and Kim, did but with a broader list of social capital questions. Such a methodology could minimize the selection effect biases and maximize the benefits from New Urban design.[73]

Notes

1. *New Urban News,* 2001, 6(7), although far more developments claim to be New Urbanist.

2. The author is grateful for the assistance of Liz Moderi in tracking down many of the articles cited in this article. See Plas, J. M., and Lewis, S. E. "Environmental Factors and Sense of Community in a Planned Town." *American Journal of Community Psychology,* 1996, 24(1), 109–143; Nasar, J. L. *The Evaluative Image of the City.* Thousand Oaks, Calif.: Sage, 1998; Duany, A., and Plater-Zyberk, E. *Suburban Nation: The Rise of Sprawl and the Decline of the American Dream.* New York: North Point Press, 2000. For a countertake on this, see Talen, E. "The Social Goals of New Urbanism." *Housing Policy Debate,* 2002, 13(1), 165–188. Talen's textual analysis of the twenty-seven principles in the *Charter of the New Urbanism* shows that none explicitly focus on community (other than some descriptive statements about how these

principles might improve community). But—given that New Urbanists' charter principles by their nature focus on design, in the hope that strong design leads to a strong and social community—it seems quite understandable that community plays a supporting and not a starring role.

3. See Burt, R. S. *Structural Holes: The Social Structure of Competition*. Cambridge, Mass.: Harvard University Press, 1992; and Burt, R. S. "Contingent Value of Social Capital." *Administrative Science Quarterly,* 1997, *42,* 339–365.

4. An international social science literature search found 20 articles on "social capital" prior to 1991, 109 between 1991 and 1995, and 1,003 between 1996 and March 1999. Winter, I. "Major Themes and Debates in the Social Capital Literature: The Australian Connection." In I. Winter (ed.), *Social Capital and Public Policy in Australia*. Melbourne: Australian Institute of Family Studies, 2000.

5. As with other forms of capital, not all forms of social capital are interchangeable. Fleeting social ties (weak ties) and deep personal relationships are both forms of social capital, but the former type is much better for finding a job and much worse for social support.

Social capital, again like other forms of capital, can be used for negative purposes. Chemistry (a form of human capital) can be used to build a useful new polymer or to construct weapons. Similarly, although most social capital is put to positive purposes, it could be used to organize either disaster relief aid or a con game.

One clear difference between social capital and financial capital is that the former is strengthened with use and atrophies with disuse, whereas the latter compounds when unused but disappears when used.

6. For greater detail about what societal goods social capital predicts, see section four in Putnam, R. D. *Bowling Alone: Collapse and Revival of American Community*. New York: Simon & Schuster, 2000.

7. Putnam (2000).

8. Also called "traditional neighborhood design."

9. It is interesting to note that the cul-de-sac, although potentially lengthening a pedestrian trip, is often cited by its residents as a great vehicle for meeting their immediate neighbors. Brown, B. B., and Werner, C. W. "Social Cohesiveness, Territoriality, and Holiday Decorations: The Influence of Cul-de-Sacs." *Environment and Behavior,* 1985, *17,* 539–565; Kim, J. "Creating Community: Does the Kentlands Live up to Its Goals?" *Places, Quarterly Journal of Environmental Design,* 2000, *13*(2), 48–55.

10. See, for example, the debate about whether Otay Ranch in the San Diego suburbs was New Urbanist, given its six-lane access road, or whether Laguna West (a highly regarded development initially designed by one of the fathers of New Urbanism, Peter Calthorpe) near Sacramento had strayed from its roots. Egan, T. "A Development Fuels a Debate on Urbanism." *New York Times,* June 14, 2002, p. A16. Specifically, there is debate about whether some of the communities examined in this article are New Urbanist—for example, Harbor Town (built by a developer trying to recapture the feeling of an older Southern neighborhood rather than as a New Urbanist town, despite many such features), the Utah subdivision examined by Barbara Brown (which has some New Urbanist design elements, but not others), Diggs Town (designed by Ray Gindroz, a later leader of New Urbanism, but, according to some, relying more on Oscar Newman's principles of "defensible space" than New Urbanist design), the Washington Elms redesign (also potentially based more on Newman than New Urbanism), and so on.

11. The HOPE VI program began as a demonstration in 1992 and originally focused primarily on mixed-income and lower-density development. More recently, designs have increasingly focused on adopting New Urbanist principles.

12. "Sand gardens" appeared intermittently throughout New England in the 1890s, with swings and sand piles. By 1904, Los Angeles became the first city to establish a Playground and Recreation Department. Two years later, the Playground Association of America was founded to facilitate organized, structured, and controlled play for urban youth in municipal playgrounds.

13. The Garden City movement was based on a book written approximately three decades earlier: Howard, E. *Tomorrow: A Peaceful Path to Real Reform.* London: S. Sonnenschein, 1898.

14. See "Ethnic Diversity Grows, Neighborhood Integration Lags Behind," a report of the Mumford Center at the State University of New York at Albany, Apr. 3, 2001, showing that residential segregation persists, particularly between blacks and whites, in cities and suburbs nationwide according to the 2000 census.

15. Comment made at the Exploring (New) Urbanism Conference at Harvard's Loeb School of Design, March 1999. It is possible that Duany meant a *common* syntax of architecture rather than a shared one since the HOPE VI architectural style probably draws much more heavily from an upper-middle-class architectural palette.

16. The HOPE VI projects, in addition to mixing incomes, contain far fewer subsidized housing units than the housing projects they replace. Those displaced from the HOPE VI sites are typically given vouchers to find housing elsewhere. This article focuses on the social capital impact of HOPE VI design, but a full social capital cost-benefit analysis would examine not only the social capital and bridging social capital created at the new HOPE VI site but also the social networks displaced by the development. Little research has been done on displaced social networks, but Kingsley and colleagues have examined where those displaced from the HOPE VI site moved to; Kingsley, G. T., Johnson, J., and Pettit, K.L.S. "HOPE VI and Section 8: Spatial Patterns in Relocation." (Prepared for the Office of Public and Indian Housing, U.S. Department of Housing and Urban Development.) Washington, D.C.: Urban Institute, 2001. See also Larry Keating's article critical of the social networks among residents of Techwood/Clark Howell Homes who were displaced by Atlanta's Centennial Place HOPE VI development; Keating, L. "Redeveloping Public Housing: Relearning Urban Renewal's Immutable Lessons." *Journal of American Planning Association,* Autumn 2000, 66(4), 384–397.

17. Four New Urbanist projects near the nation's capital did recently manage to build 30,000–55,000 square foot grocery stores, but this is the exception; *New Urban News,* July–Aug. 2001, 6(5). A Portland development also managed to fit in a Home Depot (166,000 square feet); *New Urban News,* Apr. 2001, 6(3). The obstacles are twofold: few "big box" retailers are willing to abandon their fondness for automobile-friendliness and large parking lots; and the scale of such a store, unless it is sited on the periphery, is hard to work into a New Urbanist development without compromising the community's character.

18. New Urban News, 2001, 6(8).

19. See Iovine, J. V. "Boom v. Bungalow in Seaside." *New York Times,* July 10, 1997, p. C1.

20. See Riesman, D. *The Lonely Crowd: A Study of the Changing American Character.* New Haven: Yale University Press, 1961; Whyte, W. H. *The Organization Man.* New York: Simon and Schuster, 1956.

21. Gans, H. J. *The Levittowners: Ways of Life and Politics in a New Suburban Community.* New York: Vintage, 1967.

22. Bloom, N. D. *Suburban Alchemy.* Columbus: Ohio State University Press, 2001.

23. It is ironic that Celebration's political engagement seems to have occurred in spite of the Disney Corporation's planning, not because of it. The latest example is residents' engagement in opposition to Disney's plan to add one thousand hotel rooms to Celebration's master plan; Tobin, T. "A 'Real Town' Revolt." *St. Petersburg Times,* July 28, 2002.

24. One can similarly understand "selection effects" among those who live in a standard suburban subdivision (sometimes used in comparison with a New Urbanist community). The standard suburb is likely to disproportionately attract those valuing their privacy, since the design leads to less social interaction (with more time in a car, less time spent walking, a larger lot size, and so on).

25. Bloom (2001).

26. "Insights from the Front Porch: Creating Better Communities." (Working draft.) Princeton, N.J.: Looney Ricks Kiss, July 16, 2002, p. 37.

27. The author knows of no randomized housing example. Xav Briggs, in evaluating a Yonkers, N.Y., experiment that enabled inner-city minorities to apply for vouchers to live in

a suburb, had to try to construct a representative control group through snowball sampling; the methodology is described in Briggs, X. "Brown Kids in White Suburbs: Housing Mobility and the Many Faces of Social Capital." *Housing Policy Debate,* 1998, *9*(1), 177–221. A scientific control group would be much tougher to create for a New Urbanist town where new residents are not all coming from the same neighborhood.

28. There is reason to believe in general that incoming residents of a New Urban community were not especially engaged, in civic terms, in their prior neighborhood; if they were, they would be giving up more by moving.

29. The phenomenon takes its name from Western Electric's Hawthorne plant in Chicago, where production increased between 1927 and 1932 because workers increased their productivity as a result of being singled out to take part in the experiment, rather than because of any of the productivity-enhancing methods that were tested.

30. The studies mentioned on the impact of heterogeneity, commuting time, and density are all with large sample sizes and on communities that have been around for a long time and thus avoid the "early in the game" and Hawthorne-effect problems already mentioned. There may still be selection effects in that more civic residents choose to live in a dense or urban environment. Moreover, they are not as directly on point as the studies specific to New Urbanism in the next section of this article.

31. New Urbanist developments tend to command a premium per square footage of living space. See, for example, Eppli, M., and Tu, C. *Valuing the New Urbanism.* Washington, D.C.: Urban Land Institute, 1999, showing that the eight New Urbanist communities studied commanded a 4–25 percent price premium. This price premium may be a short-term trend, as interest in New Urbanism exceeds the available supply, or it may be longer-term market validation that potential residents believe a New Urbanist town is a more livable community. Regardless of the explanation, this price premium has diminished the ability of New Urbanist communities to attract socioeconomic diversity. The experience of "new towns" is also instructive: built a generation ago with population density similar to that of New Urbanism (Columbia, Maryland, as an example) and consciously seeking income and ethnic diversity, they have shown limited ability to achieve this diversity until several decades later as the housing stock ages. See Forsyth, A. "Irvine, Columbia, and The Woodlands: Planning Lessons from Three U.S. New Towns of the 1960s and 1970s." Journal of the American Planning Association, forthcoming.

32. Campbell, D. E. "Getting Along Versus Getting Ahead: Contextual Influences on Motivations for Collective Action." Thesis, Government Department, Harvard University, 2002. Prior to Campbell's thesis, there were two findings. On the one hand, a rapidly growing body of economics literature found less social capital of various sorts in more ethnically heterogeneous communities, controlling for all the standard factors such as race, income, education, marital status, and so on; see for instance Alesina, A., Baqir, R., and Easterly, W. "Public Goods and Ethnic Divisions." *Quarterly Journal of Economics,* 1999, *114*(4), 1243–1284, showing that public goods expenditure is inversely related to an area's ethnic heterogeneity. Alesina and La Ferrara find group participation lower when ethnic, racial, and income heterogeneity are higher; Alesina, A., and La Ferrara, E. "Participation in Hetero-geneous Communities." *Quarterly Journal of Economics,* 2000, *115*(3), 847–904. The same researchers also show trust is lower when racial and income heterogeneity is higher; Alesina, A., and La Ferrara, E. "Who Trusts Others?" *Journal of Public Economics,* forthcoming. Costa and Kahn show that group participation is lower when ethnic, racial, and especially income heterogeneity is higher; Costa, D. L., and Kahn, M. E. "Understanding the Decline in Social Capital, 1952–1998." National Bureau of Economic Research working paper 8295, 2001. Glaeser and colleagues find that trust is higher among Harvard undergraduates when race and nationality are the same; Glaeser, E., Laibson, D., Scheinkman, J., and Soutter, C. "Measuring Trust." Quarterly Journal of Economics, 2000, *115*(3), 715–1090. Harris and colleagues show the state spending on education in this country is lower when the share of elderly is rising; Harris, A. R., Evans, W., and Schwab, R. "Education Spending in an Aging America." *Journal of*

Public Economics, 2001, *81*(3), 449–472. Luttmer claims that support for welfare spending in the United States is higher if a greater share of welfare recipients are from their own racial group; Luttmer, E. "Group Loyalty and the Taste for Redistribution." *Journal of Political Economy,* 2001, *109*(3), 500–528. Poterba asserts that state spending on education is lower in the United States when the share of elderly is rising and when they are from a different racial group than school children are; Poterba, J. "Demographic Structure and the Political Economy of Public Education." *Journal of Policy Analysis and Management,* 1997, *16*(1), 48–66. Vigdor finds a lower U.S. Census response rate in counties where ethnic heterogeneity is higher; Vigdor, J. "Community Composition and Collective Action: Analyzing Initial Mail Response to the 2000 Census." Unpublished manuscript, Duke University, 2001. Karlan finds lower NGO loan default rates in Peru with higher cultural homogeneity; Karlan, D. "Social Capital and Group Banking." Unpublished manuscript, Massachusetts Institute of Technology, 2002. La Ferrara shows that income inequality reduces group membership in Tanzania; La Ferrara, E. "Inequality and Group Participation: Theory and Evidence from Rural Tanzania." CEPR discussion paper no. 2433, 2002. Lindert finds that income inequality across OECD countries explains reduced expenditures on social programs; Lindert, P. "What Limits Social Spending?" *Explorations in Economic History,* 1996, *33*(1), 1–34. Miguel and Gugerty show that lower schools were of lower quality and less well funded, and water well maintenance was worse, in more ethnically heterogeneous communities in Kenya; Miguel, E., and Gugerty, M. K. "Ethnic Diversity, Social Sanctions, and Public Goods in Kenya." Unpublished manuscript, University of California, Berkeley, 2002. Costa and Kahn show that the desertion rate was higher in the U.S. Civil War union army when age and occupational diversity in the army "company" was greater; Costa, D. L., and Kahn, M. E. "Cowards and Heroes: Group Loyalty in the American Civil War." National Bureau of Economic Research working paper 8627, 2001. Goldin and Katz find that high school expansion historically was greatest in the United States where income, ethnic, and religious homogeneity were greater; Goldin, C., and Katz, L. "Human Capital and Social Capital: The Rise of Secondary Schooling in America, 1910 to 1940." *Journal of Interdisciplinary History,* 1999, vol. 29, 683–723. This list was compiled by Dora L. Costa and Matthew E. Kahn, in "Civic Engagement and Community Heterogeneity: An Economist's Perspective" (prepared for the Conference of Social Connectedness and Public Activism, Harvard University, May 2002). That paper also found that ethnic heterogeneity explained the lower voting rate in California primaries and elections; and that volunteering, membership, and trust among those age twenty-five to fifty-four were lower in heterogeneous communities, especially with high wage inequality.

Eric Oliver's research represented the other pole, showing how diversity can enhance civic engagement. Using a five-part measurement—attending community board meetings, attending voluntary association meetings, voting in local elections, contacting local officials, and engaging in informal civic activity—he found that more economically heterogeneous and well-off suburbs showed a higher level of civic engagement than more economically homogeneous communities. His results are consistent with a "conflict model" of political participation that anticipates a higher level of political engagement where people anticipate clear community-level conflict concerning political outcomes. The results combined 1990 census data with the 1990 American Citizen Participation Survey. See Oliver, J. E. "The Effects of Metropolitan Economic Segregation on Local Civic Participation." *American Journal of Political Science,* 1999, *43*(1).

Campbell notes that increased diversity may or may not increase voting, since it is both a civic norm and a self-interested act; voting tends to be highest both in the most diverse communities (where people vote to "get ahead") and the most heterogeneous ones (where people vote to "get along") (Campbell, 2002).

33. Putnam (2000), p. 213.

34. The survey data were collected through a comprehensive twenty-five-minute phone survey of thirty thousand Americans in forty communities. The survey was conducted under the auspices of the Saguaro Seminar: Civic Engagement in America project of the John F. Kennedy School of Government at Harvard University, funded by the Ford Foundation and a

consortium of some thirty community foundations and other local funders. These survey data are available at www.ropercenter.uconn.edu/scc_bench.html.

35. Williamson, T. "Sprawl, Politics, and Political Participation: A Preliminary Analysis." *National Civic Review,* 2002, *91*(3). Kevin Leyden, in a much smaller survey of 750 residents in Galway City, Ireland, found that those in more walkable neighborhoods were more likely to know their neighbors, participate politically, trust others, and socialize with friends in pubs or in each other's homes. The results controlled for age, children at home, extent of television watching, religious attendance, years in neighborhood, level of education, and strength of involvement with a political party; Leyden, K. "Social Capital, Suburbia, and Traditional Neighborhoods: Does Neighborhood Design Matter?" Under review, *Journal of the American Planning Association.* Jack Nasar found somewhat to the contrary that residence high-density was unrelated to sense of community; Nasar, J. "Neo-Traditional Development, Auto-Dependency and Sense of Community." In M. Amiel, R. Bertrand, and J. Vischer (eds.), *Proceedings of the 28th Conference of the Environmental Design Research Association,* Edmond, Okla.; Environmental Design Research Association, 1997, pp. 39–43. Lance Freeman found that residential density alone didn't predict larger neighborhood social networks, but reducing the percentage of residents driving alone did; Freeman, L. "The Effects of Sprawl on Neighborhood Social Ties: An Explanatory Analysis." *APA Journal,* Winter 2001, *67*(1), 69–77.

36. Notably, high density alone, even in conjunction with public transportation, does not lead fewer residents to drive; in three well-regarded "new towns" (having density in accordance with New Urbanist principles) a higher percentage of residents drive to work alone than the relevant state averages (Forsyth, forthcoming). New Urbanist residents who drive to work have a greater choice of routes from the grid layout (which depends far less on common arterial feeder roads), but this benefit in reducing commuting time may, in some cases, be offset by the fact that narrow roads and higher density lengthen the time it takes to access a main highway.

37. Rob Steuteville of the New Urban News believes that the "New Urban" community studied is more a hybrid than true New Urbanist for two primary reasons. First, it fails the "Popsicle" test (at least until the town center is built) since a kid could not currently walk to get a Popsicle while avoiding fast-moving cars. Second, the scale is too small to create alternative "streetscapes" amid the standard subdivision into which the "New Urban" community is interwoven (Steuteville's comments are from an e-mail to the author, July 30, 2002). However, the choice of community helped avoid selection effects, as explained in the text; Brown, B. B., and Cropper, V. L. "New Urban and Standard Suburban Subdivisions: Evaluating Psychological and Social Goals." *APA Journal,* Autumn 2001, *67*(4), 402–419.

38. Brown believes that the commercial center, when built, may not lead to much of an increase in foot traffic since it will be sited both on the lowest point of hilly terrain and just off the freeway access road, inviting car trips rather than pedestrian traffic. It is possible that the retail establishments themselves, however, will foster greater opportunity to see neighbors (private correspondence with author, July 12, 2002).

39. Brown attributes these results to the infancy of the New Urbanist neighborhood; informal socializing changed rather rapidly while neighborhood attachment took longer (private correspondence with author, July 12, 2002).

40. Adjusted means for neighboring behaviors were 0.20 for standard suburban subdivision versus 0.14 for the New Urban community, significant at p < .05 (Brown and Cropper, 2001).

41. For example, the New Urban community had higher levels of education and income, both differences that would have driven a higher level of social capital in the New Urban community independent of any impact of the community's design (Brown and Cropper, 2001). However, Brown indicates that the results on neighboring still hold, even controlling for income and education (private correspondence with author, July 30, 2002).

42. Kim (2000). Kentlands and Orchard Village had fairly similar demographics, although Kentlands residents' scores were boosted by a higher percentage of residents planning on staying indefinitely, a higher percentage of stay-at-home mothers, and a higher percentage of

members of the long civic generation (those born prior to 1931). Orchard Village's scores were elevated by residents with longer average length of residency (5.4 years vs. 3.7 years for Kentlands) and a slightly higher percentage of homeowners (95.7 percent vs. 87.5 percent in Kentlands). The response rates of 44 percent in Kentlands and 37.2 percent in Orchard Village were relatively similar. Kim, J. "Sense of Community in Neotraditional and Conventional Suburban Developments: A Comparative Case Study of Kentlands and Orchard Village." Dissertation, University of Michigan, 2002.

43. The mean number of "chance encounters with residents from other sections" was 3.92 for Kentlands and 3.49 for Orchard Village, significant at p < .001. The mean for participation in community activities was 3.68 for Kentlands and 3.49 for Orchard Village, significant only at the p < .05 level (Kim, 2002). These differences are only modest. The lower level of chance encounters in Orchard Village likely results from a less walkable community and a lack of public spaces that encourage congregating.

44. Kim suggested that these were not statistically significant since there was still significant social interaction among Orchard Village cul-de-sac residents, and that Orchard Village still demonstrated significant social support (Kim, 2002).

45. "Portland Neighborhood Survey: Report on Findings from Zone 2: Orenco Station." Jan. 20, 2002. The interviews were done face-to-face by trained graduate students and achieved a response rate of 38 percent in Orenco Station. See also Podobnik's article in this issue of the *National Civic Review.*

46. For example, 95 percent of Orenco Station residents were white; the proportion was 44 percent in northeast Portland. The median annual income of Orenco residents was $63,000, $27,000 in northeast Portland. Orenco residents had lived in their community for 1.5 years on average, compared to 7.8 in the comparison sample. These demographic differences alone could have generated substantially different social capital results. Alarmingly, despite Orenco's marketing itself as a diverse community, 65 percent of Orenco residents expressed satisfaction with the existing level of diversity and 83 percent of the respondents were satisfied with the existing age-level diversity, despite a majority of the population being over age forty; "Portland Neighborhood Survey" (2002).

47. "Insights from the Front Porch: Creating Better Communities." (Working draft.) Princeton, N.J.: Looney Ricks Kiss, July 16, 2002. The report notes that although Harbor Town "was not specifically or consciously designed using New Urbanist principles, it contains many New Urbanist elements, which includes a mixed-use town center, traditional neighborhood streetscapes that invite walking, neighborhood squares, and a variety of housing types situated on small lots" (Preface, p. 2). Their conclusions drew on a postoccupancy evaluation of Harbor Town based on a forty-six-question mail survey sent to all 1,592 Harbor Town households (from which they got a 21 percent response rate); interviews with seven apartment residents and fourteen homeowners, and seven original developers of Harbor Town; a focus group of eleven children, ages five to fourteen, in the Harbor Town Montessori School; and direct observation, at varied times of the weekday and weekend in retail areas and public spaces, of how residents interacted with their environment. Interestingly, Harbor Town residents believe they live in a diverse community; but residents are overwhelmingly white (89 percent) compared to neighboring Memphis (55 percent), and almost two-thirds of Harbor Town residents had annual income of $75,000 or greater. Three quarters of residents did not have children (probably resulting from fact that the community was not marketed to children owing to lack of such infrastructure at the time the site was built).

48. Ross, A. *The Celebration Chronicles.* New York: Ballantine, 1999; "Insights from the Front Porch" (2002).

49. The authors do not reveal all the demographics of Riverwood Farms, so one cannot assess how comparable it is. They do note similar housing prices, and that Riverwood had a much higher percentage of families with children (55 percent, versus 17 percent in Harbor Town). They received responses to their mail survey from 110 house residents and 36 apartment

dwellers in Harbor Town and 161 Riverwood residents. Both towns had a 21 percent response rate ("Insights from the Front Porch," 2002).

50. Although 85 percent of respondents in both communities labeled themselves as outgoing, Riverwood respondents socialized less with neighbors than Harbor Town's. The average Riverwood respondent knew eighteen neighbors, and some knew none, whereas the average Harbor Town respondent knew twenty-six of his or her neighbors, and all Harbor Town residents knew at least two neighbors. Both communities were close in the number of neighbors visited: seven for Riverwood and eight in Harbor Town. Residents in both towns reported five close neighborhood friends on average (Insights from the Front Porch, 2002).

51. The survey of households, which the authors label "fairly professional" (p. 257), received 268 responses, or more than 50 percent of households settled at the time of the survey; Franz, D., and Collins, C. *Celebration, U.S.A.* New York: Holt, 1999.

52. Sixty stamped and addressed letters were "lost" in a specific geographic area: twenty in phone booths (if applicable), twenty in stores, and twenty on public walkways. The lost letters tried to cover the downtown core of each area, a suburb, and a low-income inner-city area, where applicable. All U.S. letters were addressed to a post office box in Des Moines, Iowa; all Canadian and international letters were addressed to a post office box in Brandon, Manitoba. Full information on the procedure is available at http://web.mit.edu/knh/www/lostletter/lostletter.html.

53. Private e-mail correspondence with author, July 15, 2002.

54. HUD (the U.S. Department of Housing and Urban Development) recommends one-third of new units for public housing, one-third for tax-credit or subsidized housing, and a third for market-rate or homeownership housing; (HUD, "FY 2001 HOPE VI Demolition and Revitalization NOFA." Washington, D.C.).

55. "Old residents" refers to those living at the site prior to the HOPE VI renovation.

56. Pollner, L. "The HOPE VI Program: Developing Social Capital and Community in Public Housing." Unpublished paper submitted for API 420: Social Capital and Public Affairs, Kennedy School of Government, May 22, 2002. Pollner conducted detailed conversations with only ten residents, but the sample was representative of community segments in both developments, and if anything it tended to oversample those heavily involved in their community. Pollner makes clear that without any baseline measurement, it is impossible to determine whether the low level of interaction and involvement is higher or lower than it would have been without this development. Bridging social capital aside, Pollner did find that the physical design made residents more willing to take responsibility for their housing units and take pride in where they lived. Some residents got actively involved in their community (serving on tenant task forces), but most did not; "Residents across all categories—market rate and subsidized, new and old—noted that it was difficult to meet people and to get other residents to participate in more formal community activities" (Pollner, 2002, p. 11). Pollner's results are consistent with the less scientific outcomes reported in "A Mission to Share Address Is All Some Have in Common," *Boston Globe,* June 8, 2001, p. B1.

Pollner's findings are also consistent with the literature, pre-HOPE VI, showing the difficulty of developing bridging social capital, even in a model mixed-income housing site. For example, James Rosenbaum and colleagues found only superficial bridging relationships across race and income being formed at Chicago's Lake Parc Place (Rosenbaum, J. E., and others. "Lake Parc Place: A Study of Mixed-Income Housing." *Housing Policy Debate,* 1998, vol. 9, no. 4, 703–740). Brophy and Smith found limited ability to create bridging social capital at seven successful mixed-income developments, including two in Boston. The two Boston sites (Harbor Point and Tent City) and Ninth Square (in Oakland), which attracted 26 percent, 37 percent, and 28 percent of market-rate residents respectively, had minimal interaction between the subsidized and market groups, and Harbor Point tensions led to automobile vandalism (Brophy, P. C., and Smith, R. N. "Mixed-Income Housing: Factors for Success." *Cityscape,* 1997, vol. 3, no. 2, 3–32).

57. Pollner (2002), p. 23.

58. Pollner (2002), p. 13.

59. Quoted in Briggs (1998), p. 188.

60. *HOPE VI: Community Building Makes a Difference.* Feb. 2000. Prepared for the U.S. Department of Housing and Urban Development. The book does not focus on bridging social capital.

61. The analysis of this project comes from Bothwell, S. E., Gindroz, R., and Lang, R. E. "Restoring Community Through Traditional Neighborhood Design: A Case Study of Diggs Town Public Housing." *Housing Policy Debate,* 1988, 9(1), 89–114.

62. Bothwell, Gindroz, and Lang (1988), p. 108.

63. The site was remodeled along lines consistent with New Urbanism and thus affords an opportunity to assess the impact of some of these design elements, even though no one at the time labeled it a New Urbanist remodeling.

64. It may have been due to independent factors such as the nationwide drop in crime occurring at this time.

65. Siegel, L. "Washington Elms and Social Capital." Paper presented for API-420, Kennedy School of Government, spring 2002.

66. See www.ksg.harvard.edu/saguaro/communitysurvey.

67. One HUD official indicated that these sites rarely have a common place to obtain mail since it might serve as a vestige of the indignities of prior public housing.

68. The demographics of the site can substantially drive the opportunity for a common facility to create bridging relationships. For example, Charlotte's First Ward Place/Autumn Place (formerly Earle Village) has a community center with indoor and outdoor play space for children. This is theoretically a natural setting for bridging relationships to occur, yet there are no market-rate residents in First Ward/Autumn Place with children.

69. For example, in Atlanta's Centennial Park (formerly Techwood/Clark Howell Homes), 74 percent of subsidized residents wanted to live there five years or more, but only 23 percent of market-rate residents. Part of this transience is surely driven by the high percentage of students in market-rate units, but it nonetheless affects the ability to build social networks (Abt Associates. "Case Study Interim Assessment of the HOPE VI Program: Case Study of Techwood Homes and Clark Howell Homes in Atlanta, Georgia." Final report. Mar. 23, 2001.)

70. Seventy-five percent of residents had lived at Atlanta's Centennial Park for twelve months or less (Abt Associates (2001).

71. Witness Atlanta's Centennial Park, which has so far allowed only a residents' association for the entire Centennial Park complex, as opposed to the managers of Seattle's Holly Place, who have refused to furnish a list of subsidized-unit residents to those residents who want to start a separate association among the subsidized-unit people. The Holly Place managers, however, did agree to notify new subsidized-unit residents of the existence of this public housing resident association and to tell new residents how to contact them.

72. Researchers would need to control for how long people have lived in the community since it often takes time to develop civic roots.

73. None of the approaches suggested for a new New Urbanist site address the concentration effect issue, since it is presumably easier to build social capital in a place where most people want to be social.

Thomas H. Sander is the executive director of the Saguaro Seminar: Civic Engagement in America project at the John F. Kennedy School of Government, Harvard University.

Sprawl, Politics, and Participation: A Preliminary Analysis

Thad Williamson

Advocates of smart growth and other policies intended to constrain urban sprawl increasingly cite a desire to rebuild community as a primary objective of, and rationale for, reshaping America's built environment. Authors Kaid Benfield, Jutka Terris, and Nancy Vorsanger write in their fine book *Solving Sprawl* that "smart growth helps restore a sense of community by building more compact neighborhoods that are walkable, with sidewalks and safe crossings as well as home and shop entrances close enough to the street to be convenient and inviting."[1] Recent publications of the Congress for the New Urbanism stress themes of "building social capital" and "reviving community" in making the case for pedestrian-friendly places modeled on a small town downtown, not on a strip mall.

These claims by New Urbanist scholars and their allies have an intrinsic plausibility; a place that looks and feels like a coherent community should help produce citizens who are better able to identify with where they live and are more engaged in civic and political life. New Urbanists can also point to a handful of studies that seem to reinforce these claims. Perhaps most impressively, Robert Putnam's analysis of national data on civic participation concluded that a ten-minute increase in the average commuting time of a locality is associated with roughly a 10 percent decline in the rate of civic participation in that locale.[2]

The research on which this article is based has been supported in part by the Multidisciplinary Program on Inequality and Social Policy at the Kennedy School of Government, sponsored by the National Science Foundation. This article relies on the restricted-use version of the 2000 Social Capital Community Benchmark Survey conducted by the Saguaro Seminar at the Kennedy School of Government and available through the Roper Center. I would like to thank Christopher Jencks, Katherine Newman, Eric Oliver, Robert Putnam, Ann Forsyth, and several graduate student colleagues for comments and advice on earlier versions of this research, and Tom Sander for specific comments on this article.

Other scholars of American civic life, however, have been less impressed with the strength of the existing evidence. J. Eric Oliver, in his book *Democracy in Suburbia,* notes "most assertions about suburban civic life are based on either pure speculation or case studies of individual places done in the 1950s and 1960s."[3] Oliver's analysis of data on local political participation in American communities found that smaller cities as well as economically diverse cities are more likely to have a rich civic and political life. But Oliver also concluded that after controlling for socioeconomic composition, "there are few remaining social behaviors that systematically vary with a community's land use."[4] What is most damaging about American-style suburbanization, Oliver suggests, is not that more Americans now live in a bedroom community but that Americans are increasingly geographically segregated, especially by class, producing a society in which denizens of a high-income suburb need never deal with the problems of poorer citizens concentrated in older urban neighborhoods.

Oliver does not completely shut the door on claims that the geographic and physical features associated with sprawl may negatively affect civic life, but his work makes it clear that common New Urbanist hypotheses about this possible impact need to be subjected to much closer scrutiny. Building on both Oliver's work and that of Putnam and other scholars, I am currently engaged in a research project that picks up this task, drawing on a remarkable set of data recently collected by the Saguaro Seminar on Civic Life at Harvard University combined with data from the 1990 and 2000 national censuses as to local community characteristics. The Saguaro Seminar conducted interviews in 2000 with nearly thirty thousand Americans, 90 percent of whom live in one of forty distinct geographic settings (thirty-eight urban areas and two rural regions), about their civic and social habits. The urban regions that are part of this data set range from cities often associated with sprawl (such as Charlotte, Atlanta, and Houston) to metropolitan areas with high density (such as San Francisco). These cities vary widely in their rate of political participation; for instance, residents of the San Francisco area are more than three times as likely, compared to Houston-area residents, to belong to a political organization or to have signed a petition or attended a political demonstration in the previous twelve months. It is possible to analyze this data at multiple geographic levels, from census tract to city level, which permits a highly detailed examination of the impact of local spatial characteristics on America's civic life.

Research and commentary to date on the possible relationship between sprawl and civic behavior has suffered not only from a lack of data but also from insufficient conceptual clarity. A critical first step is to disaggregate the array of community characteristics that are often grouped together under the common label of sprawl. For instance, critics of America's suburbs have repeatedly identified certain community features as evidence of sprawl: low population density, high reliance on automobiles, and a long commuting time. But these three characteristics are not all positively correlated with one another;

residents of a higher-density city typically have a longer commuting time (probably because of congestion) than residents of a low-density city, and suburban environments as a whole have only a slightly longer commuting time than a central city does. It makes little sense, then, to assume that the concerns raised by New Urbanists and others can be described as part of a unified phenomenon called sprawl. Disaggregating spatial features of a community allows the researcher to test whether specific community characteristics might have differing effects on various forms of civic participation and social capital.

In research in progress, I am examining the effects of several community characteristics on civic engagement:

- Central city residence
- Population density
- Transportation patterns
- Commuting time (for both individuals and neighborhoods)
- Neighborhood age

I use seven measures of political engagement:

1. Participation in protest-type activity
2. Petition signing
3. Attending a partisan political meeting
4. Belonging to a group engaged in local reform efforts
5. Belonging to a political organization
6. Interest in politics
7. Voting in national elections

I also am testing the impact of various community characteristics on additional measures of social capital, such as public meeting attendance, group membership, friendship ties, and social trust; as well as satisfaction with one's community and self-reported individual well-being. It is important to consider multiple kinds of political participation (confrontational nonelectoral participation, nonconfrontational nonelectoral participation, and electoral participation) as well as goods other than political participation; surely a high degree of civic and political engagement is not the only important quality a healthy neighborhood or city should exhibit.

I offer first a brief overview of the main findings to date.

Central City Residence

American suburbs have frequently been portrayed as politically quiescent places free from the drama and conflict associated with big-city politics. This picture is in part confirmed by the Saguaro data; a simple comparison of the rate of political participation between central-city residents and suburban residents shows that central-city residents are more likely to be engaged in politics, particularly some conflict-oriented forms, and more likely to state that they are interested in politics. Indeed, in some ways this initial comparison understates the impact of suburbanization; as Eric Oliver has observed, other things being equal, one would expect suburban residents to be *more* engaged in politics than central-city residents since they tend to be better educated, own their own home, and have a higher income (all well-established predictors of individual-level political participation).

The importance of central-city residence for engagement in politics is confirmed and strengthened by multivariate analyses that control for a range of individual characteristics (age, gender, race, educational status, income, marital status, number of children in household, employment status and hours spent at work, homeownership status, television-watching habits, and whether or not one lives in the American South). The analyses reported here also control for a number of communitywide characteristics (by zip code), including the percentage of government workers in residence (a modest positive predictor of local political participation), median income, and the degree of economic and racial diversity. Finally, these analyses also include controls for individual commuting time as well as neighborhood-level commuting time (the impact of commuting is considered in its own right later).

My initial analysis shows that residence in a central-city location (as opposed to an inner suburb, an outer suburb, or a rural location) is a statistically significant predictor (at the 95 percent confidence level) of an individual's membership in a political organization, and a highly significant predictor (at the 99 percent confidence level) of voting in a national election, attending marches and demonstrations, belonging to a local reform organization, and interest in politics. Central-city residents also tend to be somewhat more likely to have signed a petition or attended a partisan political meeting in the past twelve months, although the impact of central-city residence falls short of statistical significance in these cases.

It is equally important to note, however, which forms of social capital central-city residence does *not* seem to enhance. Central-city residence has no significant impact (positive or negative) on attendance at public meetings (such as PTA events), the number of groups one belongs to, how many close friends one has, how trusting one is of other people, or how alienated one feels from a community's leadership. (Both central-city and suburban residents are less likely to trust others than rural residents, however.) The positive impact of central-city residence seems to apply specifically to political activities, not social capital more generally—and to apply particularly strongly to relatively contentious forms of political engagement.

A principal mechanism by which central-city residence has this effect appears fairly clear-cut in the data: central-city residents are more interested in politics than suburban residents are, and interest in politics is a strong predictor (naturally) of all forms of participation in politics. Perhaps more is at stake in the local politics of a large city compared to a suburb; perhaps a city has greater social and class conflict than a smaller place; perhaps the personalities associated with central-city politics are more compelling and more likely to be familiar to the public, not least because central-city politics is likely to dominate media coverage of local events in any metropolitan area. Perhaps, too, there are issues of self-selection involved in the linkage between central-city residence and increased interest in politics; people who are more interested in politics may gravitate toward a central city. I tested for this possibility by including "interest in politics" as an additional control; although adding this control dilutes the impact of central-city residence on political participation, it does not eliminate it—indeed, central-city residence remains a statistically significant predictor of belonging to a reform organization or attending a demonstration even *after* controlling for interest in politics.

Solo Commuting

We now turn to more specific community characteristics, starting with transportation patterns. The culture of the solo commuter driver in the American metropolitan area has been a top target of New Urbanist writers, and a study by Lance Freeman at Columbia University has shown that high dependence on automobile use appears to be linked to weakened neighborhood social ties.[5] Could transportation patterns be similarly linked to political participation as well as social capital more generally?

Preliminary evidence indicates that the answer is yes. Using the same battery of control variables just noted, but without controlling for central-city residence, I tested the impact of driving patterns on political participation using as a measure the percentage of commuters in a given zip code who do *not* drive themselves to work alone but instead carpool, use public transportation, bicycle, or walk. My initial analyses show that the lower the percentage of solo commuters in one's zip code, the more likely an individual is to belong to a political organization, be a part of a local reform organization, attend a partisan political meeting, attend a demonstration, sign a petition, or vote.

This finding is even more impressive when one considers that transportation use patterns are *not* a significant predictor of interest in politics. Consequently, the relationship between fewer solo drivers and greater participation in politics continues to hold even after one controls for an individual's interest in politics.

An intriguing question, of course, is *why* a transportation pattern should have this impact on political activity. One broad possibility is that the transportation pattern is in fact a proxy for the spatial layout of a metropolitan area. Another possibility is that the act of transportation itself has an impact on an individual's propensity to be engaged in politics (by making a public-transit user more aware of the diversity of one's community, for instance, or by allowing carpoolers the chance to converse with one another); another possibility is that a less-auto-dominated community permits greater accessibility to citizens who want to go to meetings or attend demonstrations. Still another possibility is that what is really driving this finding is the correlation between central-city residence (which predicts higher political participation) and mass transit use. Later in this article, I consider the results from models that simultaneously test multiple community characteristics while controlling for central-city residence.

The Mixed Blessing of Population Density

Sprawl is often technically defined as a process of urban development in which population density (residents per square mile) decreases over time, as outward development of land exceeds population increase in the metropolitan region. According to a 2001 Brookings Institution study, population density fell in 264 out of 281 American metropolitan regions between 1980 and 1999.[6] Does this reduction in density have negative implications for Americans' political engagement?

Evidence from the Saguaro survey suggests that it may—to some extent. First, it should be noted that the impact of density (if any) is not likely to be linear; we may think of a big city as a place where local politics is likely to be highly contested and organized, but Americans have also regarded the rural community or very small town as a place likely to be friendly to social capital and active participation in local affairs. To test the possible impact of population density on political engagement, I divided respondents in the Saguaro survey into five categories, ranging from very-high-density census tracts (9,999 or more persons per square mile) to very-low-density census tracts (fewer than 500 persons per square mile).

Living in a very-high-density area is a positive predictor at a statistically significant level of membership in a political organization, attending a march or demonstration, and signing a petition. This impact of very high density holds up even after one controls for central-city residence status (indicating that this effect is not simply reducible to central-city residence per se) and an individual's interest in politics. Residence in a very high density area also tends to be associated with membership in a local reform group, although the relationship falls just short of statistical significance. On the other hand, living in a very-high-density area has no significant effect on voting, attendance at partisan political meetings, or even interest in politics.

One plausible explanation for this finding is that very-high-density living facilitates political organization by reducing the relative costs of organizing; geographical proximity makes it is easier to get the word out or to find like-minded citizens. A less generous explanation is that living in a very-high-density area produces greater social tension and conflict, which in turn motivates participation in conflictual forms of politics. These possible explanations are not mutually exclusive, but it should also be noted that the finding that very high density may influence the rate of political activity is only indirectly relevant to the question of whether a sprawling suburb is more likely than a more compact suburb to promote political engagement. Those living in a low-density urban area (five hundred to three thousand persons per square mile) are generally less likely than those living in a moderate-density area (three thousand to seven thousand persons per square mile) to participate in politics, but in no instance is the effect statistically significant. What seems to matter is living in a very-high-density area (as in the middle of San Francisco or several other cities), not living in a New Urbanist paradise as opposed to Sprawlsville.

Complicating the picture even further is the fact that very high density can have negative implications for other forms of social capital. Very-high-density residence has a statistically significant negative effect on group membership and social trust and also contributes to greater feelings of alienation from one's community. Very high density also has a quite strong negative impact on citizens' subjective assessment of both their community's quality of life and their own personal happiness; initial analyses indicate that these negative effects remain largely intact even after one adds controls for the local violent-crime rate (which is positively correlated with higher density). In short, encouraging Americans to live in (or build) very-high-density communities would likely have a positive effect on engagement in certain kinds of politics—but only at the cost of making them less trusting and less happy.

Neighborhood Age

A major challenge in research on sprawl is finding an adequate way to measure the components of it, or a suitable proxy. One indicator that has been suggested as a proxy for neighborhood design is neighborhood age, measured by the median age of the housing stock in a given community. Was a neighborhood mostly built before the 1940s? Or was it mostly built in the 1970s and 1980s? In an intriguing finding, Eric Oliver notes that residing in a younger city in a Sunbelt state appears to be less conducive to local political participation than living in an older city; Oliver believes this effect is probably the result of the car-centered community design in more recently built communities. Another possibility is simply that an older neighborhood has a greater sense of neighborhood identity, and a longer history of activism. Whereas residents of a brand-new neighborhood must create civic organizations from scratch, residents of an older neighborhood can join established groups.

Broad survey-based research alone probably cannot adequately establish why an older neighborhood tends to be more conducive to civic and political participation than a younger neighborhood. The Saguaro survey data indicates quite strongly that this is so, however—and, it appears, not only in the Sunbelt region. My initial analysis indicates that (again, controlling for a battery of individual and community characteristics) residents of neighborhoods built before

1950 are significantly more likely to belong to a political organization, belong to a local reform organization, attend a partisan political event, attend a march or demonstration, vote in a national election, or attend a public meeting—even though living in such an older neighborhood does not increase one's interest in politics. These findings hold even after one controls for central-city residence status (central-city neighborhoods, naturally, tend to be older than suburban neighborhoods). Unlike high population density, an older neighborhood generates no adverse effect on measures of social trust, alienation, or personal happiness; residents of a new neighborhood, however, do tend to rate their community's quality of life higher than residents of an older neighborhood.

Much more additional research, probably involving in-depth examination of specific communities, is needed in future years to make sense of this apparent impact of neighborhood age on political participation. As it stands, this finding is consistent with the common New Urbanist view that neighborhood design in the United States changed in the postwar era in a way that damaged civic health; but it also suggests the broader value of preserving existing neighborhoods and the social capital networks that lie within them. Age has its advantages.

Commuting Time

The final suburbanization-related characteristic to consider is commuting time, both individual and at the neighborhood level. It stands to reason that people who must spend an hour or more a day commuting have less time (and perhaps less energy) for civic affairs. There is also good reason to suspect that the neighborhood-level commuting time is important; even if an individual has a short commute and plenty of time to meet with others, there may be no one else to meet with if all one's neighbors are exhausted from their daily expedition to work.

How well does commuting time predict political participation? Not as well as one might think. Longer individual commuting time has a notable negative impact on only one form of political behavior—voting—and even in this case the effect is quite weak, falling short of statistical significance. Neighborhood-level commuting time (when controlling for individual commute time) has no tangible impact on political behavior.

This is not to say that commuting has no effect on social capital, but it packs a punch outside the political arena. Long commuting time for an individual is a very strong predictor of reduced number of friends and attendance at public meetings and a modestly strong predictor of reduced social trust and reduced membership in groups. Interestingly, neighborhood-level (zip code) commuting time is also a very strong predictor of reduced social trust (stronger than individual commuting time, in fact). Finally, commuting time is closely related to an individual's subjective well-being; those people with a long commuting time tend to be both less happy personally and less happy with their community.

In short, the evidence is quite clear that a shorter commute time is strongly desirable for both human well-being and certain forms of social capital. There is little reason to believe, however, that reducing commuting time would significantly affect either Americans' interest or their participation in explicitly political activities.

Putting It All Together

We have now independently considered the impact (or lack thereof) of five types of community characteristics related to spatial organization: central-city status, transportation patterns, density, neighborhood age, and commuting time. All save for commuting have been shown to have an impact on at least some forms of political participation, but which of these community characteristics have the strongest effect?

To begin to answer this question, I have conducted preliminary analyses in which the impact of each community characteristic (some of which are correlated with one another) is tested simultaneously (controlling for the other individual and community characteristics previously noted). Perhaps surprisingly, the most consistent predictor of increased participation in politics in this combined analysis, by far, is reduced dependence on the automobile. Fewer solo commuters in one's zip code is a statistically significant predictor of membership in a political organization, membership in a local reform organization, attending a partisan political meeting, signing a petition, and attendance at public meetings—even when controlling for other community characteristics with which reduced auto dependence is highly correlated. In most cases, these relationships remain statistically significant after controlling for individual interest in politics.

This preliminary analysis thus suggests that there is good reason, from a civic point of view, to encourage forms of community design that reduce commuting time and to encourage the preservation and increased livability of both our older neighborhoods and our central cities. (The case for increased density per se, however, is much more ambiguous.) However, the biggest payoff, at least from a political participation point of view, appears to be in getting Americans out of their cars. The precise reason this is the case is open to interpretation, but the attachment of Americans to their automobiles is an apt metaphor for the privatization of Americans' way of life. Indeed, getting Americans out of their cars would probably prove an even more challenging endeavor than placing jobs closer to people or shoring up our cities.

Moreover, the substantive impact of these community characteristics on political participation and social capital should not be exaggerated. In most cases, it would take changes in the spatial environment that stretch the limits of policy plausibility (such as effecting a 10 percent reduction in the number of solo commuters, or encouraging systematic resettlement of a central-city area) to affect Americans' civic and political behavior in any tangible way. Nor are these spatial characteristics more consistent predictors of American political participation than socioeconomic characteristics. Confirming (and indeed strengthening) the conclusions of previous research by Eric Oliver, my analyses indicate that economic diversity at the local level (measured here as the propensity of poor and affluent households to live in the same zip code) is a positive predictor of interest in politics and every form of political participation considered, except voting in national elections.

These findings should be understood as preliminary results. I have relied in part on data from the 1990 census; future work will fully incorporate the latest geographic data from the 2000 census as they became available and also test these results using a variety of additional statistical techniques. The findings noted here indicate, however, that although community spatial characteristics do appear to have measurable impact on political participation, the size of the impact is not overwhelming in most cases, particularly when one considers the difficulty, from a policy point of view, of effecting large changes in the nature of America's built environment. Even if one takes the long view and suggests that the question is not whether the built environment can be changed overnight but instead whether it might be shaped over the next twenty to thirty years in ways that are more conducive to political engagement, another problem must be confronted soberly: the change likely to produce the most payoff in increasing political participation, namely, finding ways to get Americans out of their cars, is also the change likely to encounter the most spirited resistance, both from affected industries and from ordinary Americans.

Notes

1. Benfield, K., Terris, J., and Vorsanger, N. *Solving Sprawl.* Washington, D.C.: Natural Resources Defense Council, 2002.
2. Putnam, R. *Bowling Alone.* New York: Simon and Schuster, 2000.
3. Oliver, E. *Democracy in Suburbia.* Princeton: Princeton University Press, 2001, p. 4.
4. Oliver (2001), p. 152.
5. Freeman, L. "The Effect of Sprawl on Neighborhood Social Ties: An Explanatory Analysis." *Journal of the American Planning Association,* Winter 2001, pp. 67–77.
6. Fulton, W., Pendall, R., Nguyen, M., and Harrison, A. "Who Sprawls Most? How Growth Patterns Differ Across the United States." Brookings Institution, July 12, 2001. Washington, D.C.

Thad Williamson is a doctoral student in the Department of Government at Harvard University and coauthor of Making a Place for Community: Local Politics in a Global Age *(Routledge Press).*

New Urbanism and the Generation of Social Capital: Evidence from Orenco Station

Bruce Podobnik

Across the United States, efforts are under way to create socially enriching and sustainable urban communities. For developers who share these goals, New Urbanist models have emerged as being particularly promising templates. In an age when important segments of American society appear to be undergoing a process of social atomization, the perceived ability of New Urbanist projects to foster good neighborliness and trust at the residential level has become a particular selling point. Indeed, some analysts have claimed that New Urbanist projects are a perfect context for regenerating social capital in American cities. But are these expectations realistic? Are all the forms of social cohesion fostered within New Urbanist communities desirable on a broad level?

In this article, I offer preliminary answers to these questions by examining the social dynamics that have been generated in one particular New Urbanist community: Orenco Station, in Portland, Oregon. I have carried out a house-level survey in Orenco Station, as well as in two other neighborhoods in Portland. By comparing differences revealed in the surveys, I am able to show that social dynamics in Orenco Station vary in important ways from those in more typical Portland communities. Though not all the differences found in Orenco Station are completely positive, it nevertheless becomes clear that this New Urbanist community is indeed fostering a high level of social cohesion and community interaction. As such, this study lends support to the assertion that the New Urbanist community can foster generation of particular kinds of social capital in the contemporary American city.

The Life Cycle of Two Concepts

The concepts of New Urbanism and social capital have gone through somewhat similar life cycles in the academic and policy arenas. A period of quiet initial development has given way to a splash of public attention, as innovative applications revealed the power of the concepts. A bandwagon stage has followed, during which new uses for the concepts—some good and some bad—are advanced. A critical backlash against overextension has then occurred, to be followed in the end by a more stable phase in which the claims made for each concept are carefully tested and more nuanced lessons are extracted.

In the case of New Urbanism, architects such as Andres Duany and Elizabeth Plater-Zyberk carried out the initial groundbreaking work in the early 1980s.[1] Drawing on a long tradition of community-centered design, they designed the aesthetically and commercially successful town of Seaside, Florida. This early effort was followed during the later 1980s by other New Urbanist projects, many of which were designed by Peter Calthorpe. By promoting construction of high-density, multiuse, and mass-transit-oriented neighborhoods, practitioners demonstrated that a socially cohesive and environmentally sustainable community could be created in a city or suburb. This emergent architectural movement took formal shape in 1993, with creation of the Congress for the New Urbanism (CNU). Through the strong advocacy work of the CNU, New Urbanist principles have become embedded in an impressive number of projects over the last fifteen years.

New Urbanist practitioners can certainly point to impressive achievements, but the movement has also had to contend with an important critical backlash. Defenders of conventional suburban development have argued that New Urbanist projects are trying to squeeze more people onto smaller lots, thereby contravening traditional market dynamics. Social theorists, meanwhile, have expressed concern about the tendency of the New Urbanist development to be targeted toward an affluent, homogeneous population. Many environmental researchers have raised questions about New Urbanism's ability to provide a truly sustainable model for broader urban development. Though sometimes overly strident, such criticism has the healthy effect of forcing some advocates (most notably those associated with the CNU) to begin addressing potential limitations head-on. Criticism has also motivated empirical research into the on-the-ground outcomes of the New Urbanist community. With New Urbanism, in short, we are at a stage in which careful research can tease apart the beneficial and problematic dimensions of a specific project.

The concept of social capital has gone through a similar cycle of development, popularization, critique, and maturation. Independently invented at numerous times, the term refers to the bonds of familiarity and trust that can grow between people within small groups and larger communities. As people interact in a formal or informal context, the expectation is that they will generate allegiances of varying intensity that can promote individual and communal welfare. For instance, sociologists Mark Granovetter and James Coleman and others have shown that the existence of an interpersonal network can lead to improved job prospects or better educational outcomes for an individual.[2] As they and others demonstrate, the power of social capital arises not out of individually oriented, maximizing behavior but instead out of social interaction creating and sustaining bonds of familiarity and trust.

The concept of social capital came into quite extensive use in academic circles in the 1980s, but it was the work of Robert Putnam that brought the term to wide popular attention in the 1990s. His article "Bowling Alone" (which was later expanded into a book of the same title) painted a worrisome picture of an American society in which social interactions have eroded over the last few decades.[3] Evidence marshaled by Putnam depicts widespread decline in participation in groups as varied as bowling leagues, neighborhood associations, union committees, and political organizations. As individuals have stopped interacting in such a context, bonds of familiarity, goodwill, and trust have evaporated. This decline in socializing and social capital, according to Putnam, puts general civility and democracy at risk.

Putnam's work captured broad attention and spurred a flurry of new applications of the concept of social capital. In most cases, the term was used to describe beneficial ways in which social interaction can assist an individual, a community, or even an entire nation to improve its circumstances. Predictably, something of a critical reaction to this rosy-tinged bandwagon has begun to take place. Alejandro Portes, for instance, has demonstrated that social capital can be a double-edged sword. His work shows that social ties can be marshaled to accomplish good things, such as advancing people within an ethnic enclave; but they can also foster unhealthy allegiances within a gang.[4] As Putnam has also argued, social capital can have exclusionary as well as inclusionary aspects. The very same social dynamics that may foster group allegiance can also lead to an us-versus-them mentality.

The nuanced specifications that are emerging from this period of critique allow analysis of which specific kinds of social capital are fostered in a particular situation, and which are not. As I argue in this article, Orenco Station appears to be a community in which a high level of *bonding* social capital (meaning, within-neighborhood cohesion) has been generated. This is a hopeful development. It suggests that the New Urbanist community is an arena in which social engagement and interpersonal trust (that is, social capital) can be regenerated.

On the other hand, I also argue that Orenco Station has not been particularly successful, as of yet, in generating *bridging* social capital (meaning, linkage to people outside the community). There are indications in my research that many original residents of the neighborhood were resistant to integrating a more ethnically and financially diverse population into the community. Moreover, there appears to be some hostility within the neighborhood to outsiders who come to use public amenities such as a local park. By raising a cautionary point about certain exclusionary dynamics within the community, I am not trying to diminish the real achievements realized at an early stage in the Orenco Station project. With a modest effort, residents and planners in the community can work to build bridges between the community and the wider city. As with all social projects, the more we confront potential problems and work directly to counteract them, the stronger the long-term outcomes can be.

The Portland Neighborhood Survey

Before I turn to a review of specific empirical findings, it is important to describe the methodology used in my research. I also need to describe the overall characteristics of the three neighborhoods that I am comparing.[5]

The data reported here were generated by the Portland Neighborhood Survey, which is an ongoing project designed to gather information on living conditions in communities across the city. Acting as principal researcher, I have trained interviewers to administer a rather extensive questionnaire to residents in specific target neighborhoods. The interviewers for this study were college students enrolled in my Quantitative Research Methods course, which is taught at Lewis and Clark College. Once trained in the specifics of survey research, groups of students were sent out to every residence along streets in particular zones to knock on doors and solicit interviews. If a resident agreed to an interview, approximately sixty-five questions covering social, health, and environmental topics were asked. Respondents were invited to report on their personal situation, as well as conditions of the other members of the household. For instance, we asked whether the main respondent, or anyone else in the residence, participates in any formal or informal neighborhood group. Therefore, in general we collected information on each topic from more than one person in each residence where an interview was completed.

As with all survey research, there is the possibility that through door-knocking techniques nonrandom groups of people might be contacted.[6] A number of steps were taken to reduce this danger. Groups of interviewers were sent down each street on at least two days, to maximize the chance that a resident in every house would be contacted at least once (then accepting or refusing to participate in an interview). Most of the field research was done on weekends, between the hours of 11:00 A.M. and 5:00 P.M., to increase the likelihood that a representative segment of the population would be home. As it turned out, our response rate (the number of interviews completed per house contacted) in each of the three neighborhoods hovered around 40 percent. Most important, because the methodology employed was identical in each neighborhood, whatever remaining nonrandom biases crept in are probably the same across the zones. Neighborhood characteristics captured by the surveys are therefore likely to reflect real underlying differences between communities.

The three neighborhoods surveyed to date are a community in northeast Portland (surveyed in 2000), the New Urbanist development of Orenco Station (surveyed in 2001), and a community in southwest Portland (surveyed in 2002). These areas differ in many important respects, but a few key distinctions need to be highlighted.

The northeast zone is located in a long-established section of downtown Portland. It is an ethnically diverse part of the city, with a high concentration of African American, Latino, and Asian residents. This is reflected in the survey. Of the 587 people we got information on in this zone (from 199 residences), 43 percent were self-identified as white while 57 percent were from other ethnic groups. It is also one of the poorest sections of the city. In the survey results, the median monthly household income of northeast respondents was in the range of $2,000 to $2,500. This area of the city suffered in the past from a high crime rate, unemployment, and poor schools, though more contemporary concerns focus on problems such as gentrification, highway expansion, and pollution. On the other hand, the northeast zone has a strong tradition of church- and community-based organizing and is viewed as being one of the most socially dynamic areas of the city.

The community of Orenco Station differs sharply from northeast Portland in almost every respect. This new development (first opened in 1997) lies in the western suburbs, between the towns of Beaverton and Hillsboro. This area of the city has experienced rapid growth in the high-tech sector over the last two decades, which has in turn generated many high-paying jobs. Like its surrounding environs, Orenco Station is an affluent and ethnically homogeneous community. This is again reflected in the survey data. Of the 234 people we collected information on in this area (from 114 residences), 95 percent were self-identified as white and the median monthly household income was in the range $5,000 to $5,500. The most pressing problems faced in this section of the city involve coping with rapid population growth and traffic congestion. The level of social engagement in western Portland has not historically differed much from that in other suburbs, though Orenco Station stands out in this respect, as I describe later.

The final comparison zone is situated in a more established, traditional suburban section of southwest Portland. In key characteristics, it falls between the extremes of the other two neighborhoods. Of the 359 individuals for whom information was collected in this neighborhood (from 137 residences), 78 percent were white; the median monthly household income of respondents fell in the range of $3,500 to $4,000. In general, people in this area of the city are not known as being particularly socially engaged. However, a certain number of residents have recently become mobilized to contest specific urban development projects planned for the area.

In sum, we have here the ability to compare social dynamics in the New Urbanist community of Orenco Station with those in two neighborhoods of a more traditional kind, one located in Portland's central city area and the other situated in a well-established, traditional suburban zone. With this background information on the communities and survey methodology in mind, we can now turn to analysis of the specific kinds of social capital being generated within one particular New Urbanist neighborhood.

Bonding Dynamics Within Orenco Station

There is certainly no automatic link between the neighborhood in which individuals reside and the people with whom they most commonly interact. For some, acquaintances are found primarily at work or school, so there is little correspondence between their place of residence and their social network. For others, the telephone and Internet provide technological mechanisms for creating and sustaining even more deterritorialized social linkage. Still, most evidence suggests that a significant majority of Americans want to develop at least passing connections with the people they live near. One of the central goals of the New Urbanist developer is to create a physical space that fosters this kind of residential social interaction.

The core area of Orenco Station has been constructed in such a way as to increase the likelihood that residents get to know one another, and perhaps establish bonds of trust and goodwill.[7] Houses, for instance, have small private yards but are surrounded by an impressive array of public parks, sports facilities, and meeting areas. This reduction in private space and increase in public space is meant to bring people into more frequent interaction with one another. Similarly, pathways and sidewalks ensure that all residents can take a comfortable walk to shops in the town center. In addition to reducing the need to use a car to go shopping, this pedestrian-friendly design increases the likelihood of people getting to know one another while going through a regular shopping routine within the local community.

The physical design of Orenco Station differs markedly from the layout of the other two neighborhoods. In the area studied in northeast Portland, houses are arrayed in a traditional urban grid. The modest number of parks and shopping facilities found in this neighborhood are clustered in specific zones, so that most residents live further away from public amenities than their Orenco Station counterparts. Heavily traveled surface streets bisect the zone at numerous points, making it harder for northeast residents to walk to the public areas that do exist.

Residents in the southwest neighborhood live in even more of an atomized physical context. Here, private yards tend to be large, while sidewalks are often nonexistent. Parks and shops are even further removed from residential areas, so it is almost a necessity that people drive to any public meeting space. The physical design of both comparison communities, in short, serves to decrease chances for social interaction, while Orenco Station's design is meant to have the opposite effect.

So, is there evidence to suggest that differing social dynamics are being fostered in these distinct physical environments? In a word, yes. For instance, we asked respondents to describe the three best aspects of their neighborhood.

The open-ended answers were then grouped into meaningful categories (so that "friendliness," "nice neighbors," "good people," and so on were combined into a single "community friendliness" category). Once all answers were compiled, patterns emerged that differed with the neighborhood. Importantly, the most commonly cited best aspect of life in Orenco Station is some version of the community friendliness answer. Specifically, 24 percent of the Orenco Station answers referred to some aspect of community friendliness, followed next by "physical design of the community" (14 percent) and then by "proximity to stores/businesses in local area" (11 percent). In comparison, only 14 percent of responses from northeast Portland cited community friendliness as one of the three best aspects of that area, while only a very few (5 percent) of the southwest responses offered that answer. By far, the most common positive aspect cited in northeast and southwest Portland had to do with "location in wider city" (each offers relatively easy driving access to the downtown area and major sites of employment).

Two other survey questions also shed light on the general level of community friendliness found in each neighborhood. One question was, "Are people here more or less friendly than where you lived before?" Fifty-nine percent of the Orenco Station respondents said "more friendly," compared to 45 percent and 42 percent in northeast and southwest Portland. An even sharper difference emerges in response to the question, "Is there more or less of a sense of community here than in other Portland neighborhoods?" Seventy-eight percent of Orenco Station respondents said "more here," compared with 46 percent in the northeast and 32 percent in the southwest. Taken together, the evidence suggests that Orenco Station offers a significantly more congenial social atmosphere than either the central city neighborhood or the more traditional suburban zone.

If there is indeed a greater level of general friendliness in Orenco Station, is this associated with a pattern of participation in local group activity? Again, the answer seems to be yes. In the surveys, we asked respondents of all three communities to list the formal or informal neighborhood groups that anyone in the household participates in. On the broadest level, a noticeable difference can be discerned. In 40 percent of the Orenco Station homes, at least one person was reported to engage in some group activity. This compares with 31 percent and 30 percent in the northeast and southwest communities, respectively.

At a more detailed level, additional differences in the pattern of group participation emerge. For instance, by far the most common kind of group activity reported by Orenco Station residents (47 percent of responses) fell into the category of "participation in BBQs, dinners, and other informal neighborhood get-togethers." The next most frequently cited categories in Orenco Station were "homeowners associations" (26 percent) and "book clubs" (10 percent). In contrast, the most commonly cited group activities reported by northeast Portland residents were participation in "anticrime groups" (32 percent), "church groups" (26 percent), and "advocacy groups of a political, civic, or environmental nature" (14 percent). In southwest Portland, only two categories of group activity (participation in a homeowners association or an anticrime group) were cited with any frequency.

What emerges here is a picture of a New Urbanist community in which many people are actively engaging with one another in myriad informal ways. Rather than being focused primarily on structured self-protection activities such as anticrime and homeowners associations, group activities in Orenco Station appear to be geared more toward socializing for its own sake. This suggests, at least indirectly, that a higher level of trust and goodwill has been generated within this neighborhood than in the comparison communities. Such an outcome is remarkable, given that at the time of the survey residents had been living in Orenco Station for an average of only two years (compared with an average time of residence in northeast and southwest Portland of eight years each).

Of course, we need to be careful about assuming that a causal relationship exists between the physical design of Orenco Station and the kind of social bond that has grown between residents. Other survey questions reveal clearly that the people who moved into Orenco Station were often doing so because they wanted to live in a high-density, socially interactive community. This self-selection dynamic is absent in the other two communities, which may partly explain the different social outcomes. Still, whatever the original mind-set of the Orenco Station inhabitants, the fact remains that continued social engagement is occurring in the community. At this early stage in its development, Orenco Station has clearly helped generate a remarkably high level of interaction and friendliness (again, social capital) among its residents.

Building Bridges Between Orenco Station and the Wider City

It is certainly a hopeful sign that the community of Orenco Station appears to have generated strong bonding social capital. However, as urban geographer David Harvey has pointed out, there is often a tendency for a community with a strong local bond of solidarity to develop an exclusionary attitude with respect to outsiders.[8] Sociological research has further demonstrated that the danger of such an attitude emerging is heightened if the community is internally homogeneous in terms of ethnicity and socioeconomic class.

In many respects, the early stage of development of Orenco Station provided an almost ideal breeding ground for emergence of exclusionary attitudes. Again, at the time of my survey work the neighborhood was inhabited almost entirely by white, affluent professionals. Even in other respects, the neighborhood was internally homogeneous. There were few children, adolescents, or teenagers, for instance. Moreover, the carefully constructed and maintained amenities such as parks and sports facilities within Orenco Station contrasted with a relative lack of similar amenities in surrounding suburbs. In short, the setting was right for developing a strong us-versus-them mentality within the New Urbanist community.

Some evidence from my survey research indicates that a moderately exclusionary attitude did indeed grow among some of the original residents of Orenco Station. Take the issue of ethnic diversity. In all three comparison neighborhoods we asked, "How do you feel about the ethnic diversity of this neighborhood?" In Orenco Station, 65 percent of respondents replied that they were happy with the existing level of diversity (at a time when the neighborhood was 95 percent white). Only about a third of Orenco Station residents stated that they wished their community were more diverse. In contrast, in the more typical (and majority white) suburban community of southwest Portland, 52 percent of residents stated that they wished their neighborhood were more diverse. Clearly, a substantially lower proportion of Orenco Station residents expressed interest in bridging an ethnic divide than inhabitants of a comparable suburb in another part of the city.

We also posed one question to Orenco Station residents that can shed light at least indirectly on the issue of class diversity. The question was, "Should a certain number of affordable houses, designed for people with lower incomes, be built in Orenco Station?" Forty percent of respondents said no outright, while another 22 percent expressed significant reservations about the idea. Interestingly, we again found that about a third of the respondents said they would support this kind of effort to integrate the community economically.

There are other, more direct indications that some original residents of Orenco Station were resistant to any incursion of outsiders into their idyllic community. For instance, at the time of the survey one major concern of many residents was that nonresidents were entering the neighborhood to use the area's parks. Now, the parks were actually owned and maintained by the city, so it was quite appropriate for residents in surrounding neighborhoods to use them. However, some Orenco Station residents complained that nonresidents were causing littering, parking, and safety problems. In a rather intriguing conversation at an Orenco Station homeowners association meeting, various proposals were floated to address the problem, two of which were to have the association take formal ownership of the parks and hire security personnel to keep nonresidents out, and to reduce public parking around the parks to make access to them more difficult. In this conversation, which took place between approximately forty residents, no one suggested that nonresidents might be encouraged to use the parks in a way that respected local norms of behavior. (In fact, no one suggested that some Orenco Station residents might also have been engaging in less-than-perfect park etiquette.) Similar concerns have been expressed about cases in which nonresidents were found to be using local sports facilities, though because these are private property there is a clearer ability to request that nonresidents leave if they are encountered.

None of these semicritical observations are meant to suggest that, in its early stage, Orenco Station generated a strong exclusionary culture among the majority of its residents. Keep in mind that there was a healthy minority of Orenco Station residents who expressed support for greater ethnic and class diversity. The concern about the incursion of nonresidents is reflected in the other communities surveyed. For instance, many of the nonwhite people who responded to our survey in the northeast section of Portland (where gentrification is a major concern) stated that they wished fewer whites would move into that neighborhood. Meanwhile, some residents in the traditional suburban study area also expressed concern about outsiders using their parks. Indeed, it is quite remarkable that the physical and social characteristics of the early phase of the Orenco Station project did not generate an even more exclusionary attitude among residents.

Still, we must acknowledge that evidence of an exclusionary attitude emerges a bit more strongly in Orenco Station than in either comparison community. Moreover, the experience of other New Urbanist neighborhoods across the country has demonstrated that communities of this kind can become somewhat resistant to "the outsider" over time. Indeed, it is becoming increasingly clear that a key area in need of monitoring is the extent to which strong bonds of solidarity generated within a New Urbanist neighborhood can translate into an exclusionary attitude toward nonresidents.

Fortunately, there is ample evidence to suggest that many proponents of New Urbanism are embracing the challenge of fostering more inclusionary and equitable dynamics within their development. Planners affiliated with the CNU, for instance, have suggested strategies for creating stronger linkage between a New Urbanist neighborhood and the wider region within which it is located. Suggestions include organizing summer music and art festivals within the New Urbanist community, and recommendations that an association within the community become more politically engaged in citywide efforts to promote sustainability. In addition, CNU has in recent years advocated strongly for an increase in the number of New Urbanist projects geared toward central-city and less-affluent populations.

Meanwhile, back in Orenco Station there are reasons to expect that the modestly exclusionary dynamics uncovered in my research will subside over time. This is largely because the demographic and class characteristics of the community are undergoing substantial diversification. At the time of my survey work, only a core zone of pricey townhouses and condos was fully inhabited. In more recent months, new apartment complexes have opened up and a contingent of younger, less affluent, and more ethnically diverse residents has begun to move into the community. For this reason, Orenco Station is becoming an even more unique New Urbanist neighborhood, one in which internal social differences are growing rather than narrowing. Future research has to determine whether the strong bonds of solidarity generated within an initially homogeneous population break down, or whether Orenco Station's increasingly diverse population can fashion strong connections that bridge class and ethnic divides.

Notes

1. For a recent presentation of the views of these architects, consult Duany, A., Plater-Zyberk, E., and Speck, J. *Suburban Nation: The Rise of Sprawl and the Decline of the American Dream.* North Point, N.Y.: Farrar Straus and Giroux, 2000.

2. See, for instance, Granovetter, M. *Getting a Job: A Study of Contacts and Careers.* Cambridge, Mass.: Harvard University Press, 1974; and Coleman, J. "Social Capital in the Creation of Human Capital." *American Journal of Sociology,* 1988, *94,* S95–S120.

3. Putnam, R. *Bowling Alone: The Collapse and Revival of American Community.* New York: Simon & Schuster, 2000.

4. Portes, A. "Social Capital: Its Origins and Applications in Modern Sociology." *Annual Review of Sociology,* 1998, *24,* 1–24.

5. Readers wishing more detailed information on the methodology used, or on the neighborhoods examined, are encouraged to contact the author or review the Website (www.lclark.edu/~podobnik/Neighborhood_Survey.html).

6. There is some evidence to suggest that door-knocking survey techniques are actually more reliable than telephone surveys, especially in an age when telephone screening devices are finding widespread use.

7. Orenco Station has been undergoing continual expansion since its inauguration in 1997, with zones opening in distinct stages. For information on the history and current status of the development, consult the Orenco Station Website (www.orencostation.com/home.htm).

8. Harvey, D. *Justice, Nature and the Geography of Difference.* Cambridge, Mass.: Blackwell, 1996.

Bruce Podobnik is assistant professor in the Department of Sociology and Anthropology at Lewis and Clark University, Portland, Oregon.

Access to Opportunity:
The Biggest Regional Challenge

Richard J. Porth

When we were growing up in Philadelphia in the late 1950s and early 1960s, my grandfather would take us for rides in the "country." A new highway had been built connecting our city neighborhood with small towns and wide-open farmland. Even though the highway extended only about twenty miles or so outside the city line, the countryside seemed like another world to us. It didn't take very long before many of the families in our neighborhood followed the highway out of the city to new homes and communities. Most of the people who grew up in my neighborhood back then now live in suburban towns along that same highway. New black families moved into our old neighborhood. My story isn't unique. Millions of Americans in regions all over the country can tell a similar tale.

In most regions, people, jobs, and wealth were dispersed ever further out from our cities after World War II. Since 1950, population density in America's central cities has declined by 50 percent.[1] This decentralization has yielded real benefits, enabling many Americans to pursue the dream of having a single family home with a car in the driveway.

But the downside is only now being fully understood. Today, many regions are struggling with tough problems connected with decentralization. We face governance challenges in balancing the traditional authority of numerous local governments with a growing need for regionwide solutions. New environmental concerns about protecting key assets (watersheds, ridgelines, farmland, open space) require regional action. We are growing increasingly impatient with traffic congestion, but many of us oppose any proposal of a new highway or road widening. This phenomenon even has a name: the asphalt revolt. Finally, this decentralization has separated Americans along lines of race and income in many regions. It has caused severe concentration of poverty in many cities, which in turn has cut many people off from access to decent schools, jobs, and housing.

Bill Dodge, former executive director of the National Association of Regional Councils, has described a governance disconnect in American life that is becoming ever more apparent and problematic. Our formal government structures are set up at the municipal, state, and federal levels. But an increasing number of our most pressing problems exist at the neighborhood, regional, and international levels. Issues such as workforce and economic development, transportation and infrastructure investment, water supply protection, housing supply, open space and farmland preservation, and access to opportunity require regional strategies if they are to be resolved.

For example, competition in the new global economy increases the need to ensure that local public services are provided in the most cost-effective way. Is the public's money being used prudently when roads, water lines, and other public infrastructure (including schools) are built in a less-populated area while there is still underused capacity in our cities and older suburbs? Does this pattern of resource expenditure contribute to the decline of cities and older suburbs?

Many of us worry about the damage done when watersheds, ridgelines, and prime agricultural land are used for new commercial and residential developments. Some say this worry is unwarranted, but many highly productive agricultural areas, such as Lancaster County in Pennsylvania and our own Connecticut River Valley here in New England, are among the most threatened in the United States thanks to development pressures.

Traffic congestion and related issues have neared the top of the list in recent years in responses to surveys asking Americans to identify their biggest concerns. As a society, we know we have a problem, but we have no consensus on how to fix it. This situation is complicated by the fact that although most meaningful solutions require greater coordination of land use planning as well as transportation investment decisions at the regional level, in most areas land-use decisions are the exclusive responsibility of a local government.

But the greatest concern related to decentralization is that it has increased the concentration, and isolation, of low-income people in our country's urban areas. David Rusk, former mayor of Albuquerque, New Mexico, and a highly regarded commentator on cities and regions, documented this separation in his book *Cities Without Suburbs*.[2] He demonstrated a growing disparity in the city-suburb income ratio, from 1979 to 1989, in a number of regions in the Northeast and Midwest. Places like Chicago, Philadelphia, Detroit, Baltimore, and Cleveland all experienced a decline in the city-suburb income ratio during this time. But the steepest declines and lowest ratios were registered in such smaller northeastern cities as Trenton (50 percent), Hartford (53 percent), and Newark (42 percent).

In a subsequent book (*Inside Game/Outside Game*), Rusk showed that there is a racial component in this separation of rich and poor in our country.[3] Using an unweighted average for fifty-eight regions across the nation, Rusk found that only 26 percent of whites who are classified as poor under federal poverty guidelines lived in a poverty area (defined as a census tract where more than 20 percent of residents fall under the poverty line). By contrast, 54 percent of poor Latinos and 75 percent of poor blacks lived in a poverty area. In many places, this disparity is even more striking, and the concentration of poverty has grown over time. Among the fifty-eight metropolitan areas he studied, Rusk counted 421 high-poverty tracts (more than 40 percent in poverty) in 1970 and 1,179 in 1990.[4]

Ongoing concerns over traffic congestion, loss of open space and farmland, damage to watersheds and ridgelines, and additional cost to taxpayers for infrastructure and public services are all real and important ingredients in our future economic vitality and quality of life. But as argued by others before me, the biggest and toughest regional challenge—the one likely to have the greatest long-term impact on our nation's economic vitality and social fabric—is the concentration of poverty in our cities and resultant loss of access to opportunity for many Americans.

Access to Opportunity: Why Should We Care?

There are at least three easily identifiable reasons why we should care about whether some among us are denied access to opportunity, such as good schools, good jobs, and decent housing choices: (1) regional economic performance, (2) the impact of concentrated poverty, and (3) making good on America's promise.

Economic Performance: The City-Suburb Economic Link. Since the late 1980s, a number of studies have assessed the economic links between cities and their suburbs. In a recent article entitled "The Effects of Poverty in Metropolitan Area Economic Performance," Paul Gottlieb analyzes eighteen studies on city-suburb economic links, among them work by notable researchers such as Richard Voith, H. V. Savage, and Roland Benabou.[5] A number of the studies indicate a positive correlation between city and suburban per capita income or income growth, and a few find a positive correlation between cities and suburbs for population growth or for employment growth.

Gottlieb raises questions about some of the work and suggests areas for additional research. But ultimately, he writes that these studies "generally confirm the hypotheses of (1) a positive correlation between central city and suburban economic performance; (2) a positive correlation between central city and metropolitan economic performance; and (3) a positive correlation between greater spatial equality and metropolitan economic performance."[6] Gottlieb goes on to say that the studies indicate this interdependence is more complementary then competitive. In other words, cities and suburbs today are not involved in a zero sum competition (I win, you lose). A better analogy is the overused but appropriate "we are all in this together."

In my experience, these findings make sense because of how education is provided in many regions around the country. Certainly throughout much of New England and the Northeast, school districts are usually aligned with municipal boundaries. With the continuing drain of middle-income and upper-income families from our cities, the proportion of low-income students in city classrooms has steadily grown. A major factor in the performance of city schools is the high rate of poverty among its students.[7]

Some have argued that top-heavy, ineffective school administration and powerful teacher unions that focus more on teachers than students are the cause of this poor performance. This may or may not be true, depending on the city and the school district. But the mixed results being reported from state takeover of urban school districts around the country argue that the fundamental problem goes much deeper. Aside from the occasional example of heroic efforts to educate young people in a school in a poor neighborhood, generally speaking the larger the concentration of poverty-level students in any classroom, the more remote the prospects of success for many students.

Some researchers, most notably Roland Benabou, are looking carefully at this dynamic.[8] Their work is helpful in improving our understanding of the relationship between the productivity of a region's workforce and the likelihood of children getting a decent education. Because students from city schools represent a significant part of each region's workforce, the long-term economic vitality of the entire region depends on young people in a city having an opportunity to get a good education and then access to a decent job. We need all hands on deck if our regions and our nation are to stay competitive in the new global economy.

Impact of Concentrated Poverty on a Region. In an early analysis of how the growing concentration of poverty affects many cities, Mark Hughes demonstrated that such concentration leads to greater isolation of people living in poverty and therefore greater persistence of poverty.[9] It is difficult for people to move out of poverty if they don't have the physical and personal connections that help them get a decent education and then find a good job. The result is great hardship for those living in such isolated poverty. The by-products of concentrated poverty—poor schools, decaying neighborhoods, crime, high unemployment, teen pregnancy, and so on—make life very hard for even the most resilient.

Let me illustrate this with a little story. When I lived in Trenton, I coached a basketball team at the local YMCA. One day, my cousin invited me to a picnic at his home, about twenty miles up the Delaware River on the Pennsylvania side. I brought one of my players, age twelve, and his nine-year-old cousin, with me to the picnic. I picked them up at their home in a poor neighborhood in Trenton, and as we began our trip up the river it was apparent that neither of them had traveled very far beyond the edge of the city before. They both remarked on the trees and the green lawns, and as we drove through a small town they were impressed with how clean and how quiet it was. Finally, the younger one pointed to some people and asked, "Do those people speak the same language as us?" This was an eye opener for me, demonstrating the extent of the isolation of these kids and many others in our cities. It would not surprise me if kids from some of our suburbs reacted the same way on a trip into the city. This kind of separation and isolation certainly hurts all of them, and it cannot be in the best interest of our society as a whole.

The impact of this concentrated poverty can also be felt in the suburban areas and outer reaches of many metropolitan regions. Regions continue to be identified nationally and internationally by the name of their hub city. Cities remain the flagships of our regions. Increasingly, we realize that the image of a region depends in large measure on the image of its central city. When business magazines and business locators rate a metropolitan area and its business climate, they often look at social and economic conditions in the central city as a key indicator of the health of the entire region. Most regions whose central city has a high concentration of poverty are fighting an uphill battle to project an image that attracts talented people and new investment.

Myron Orfield, a Minnesota state senator and a keen observer of cities and regions, uses a series of compelling maps to demonstrate how rapid decline in cities and older suburbs places real stress on communities at the edge of the region, especially as a result of school overcrowding and strain on limited infrastructure such as roads and water and sewer service.[10] As an example, a number of the towns I serve in the Hartford region are struggling to accommodate rapid student population growth even while Hartford's school enrollment drops. Likewise, some of our towns are grappling with serious traffic congestion, one of the unforeseen consequences of their success in luring new residents and commercial development into town.

Making Good on America's Promise. As jobs, stores, educational opportunities, and other amenities continue to be dispersed further and further out, many people are denied access to them because they do not have a car. This barrier affects the young and the old, people who are disabled, and those who cannot afford an automobile.

This lack of access can affect regional economic performance, if suburban employers cannot get the workers they need. An October 2000 White House report estimated that two-thirds or more of the new jobs being created in the United States are in suburban locations. Access to these jobs, many of which are service and entry-level, is difficult for people who do not own a car, since the new job location is usually poorly served by mass transit. Many regions have instituted reverse-commute job-access transportation services, which have helped connect some people to these suburban jobs. But we are only touching the tip of the iceberg.

While many low-income people still cannot get transportation to a distant job, others struggle to learn the skills they need to get a good job because their only option for education is in a school with a high level of poverty. Developing the good work habits needed to keep a job is tougher for someone living in a neighborhood with high unemployment. Neighbors and family members with good jobs make for good role models. They are often the best source of job leads, too.

This lack of access to opportunity raises real concern about equity. An axiom of life in America is that if you work hard you can make it. Barriers to opportunity created by lack of physical and personal connections work against the basic American principle of equality of opportunity. When we work for better access to opportunity for everyone, we recommit ourselves to America's promise. It's the right thing to do.

Former U.S. Sen. Bill Bradley said it this way in a speech to the New Jersey Chamber of Commerce on Feb. 7, 1991:

> White America's frequent reaction to our cities is to move physically farther and farther away. But having moved away we cannot leave the city behind in our minds, evading its tragedies with the comforting thought that we no longer live there. . . . When we put up mental walls between our lives and the lives of our cities, we destroy the very connections that could potentially enrich and strengthen our society. When those walls are erected, they separate us less from violence than from our destiny as a nation that can lead the world by example. The higher the mental walls go, the more cities seem like prisons as America's promise of freedom, mobility and individual fulfillment drifts farther and farther away.

Reconnecting People: Public Policy Responses

The debate over which public policies work best to address the serious problems we face from separating people by income has been full and lively. In his book *New Visions for Metropolitan America,* the Brookings Institution's Anthony Downs breaks out the basic policy strategies into five categories:

1. Adjustment strategies, which do not address the root causes of the problem but offer assistance to city governments and city residents
2. Area development strategies, which include neighborhood revitalization and job-creation projects
3. Human capital development strategies, which make training and education available to residents of a poor neighborhood, whether or not they move elsewhere
4. Household mobility strategies, which assist residents of a poor neighborhood in moving out to neighborhoods and towns with more socioeconomic balance
5. Worker mobility strategies, which help residents of a poor neighborhood get to jobs outside the neighborhood, especially in suburban towns[11]

Bruce Katz, the head of the Center on Urban and Metropolitan Policy at the Brookings Institution, offers some recommendations in a report called "Reviving Cities: Think Metropolitan."[12] It suggests a number of policies that could be enacted at the state level and in Washington, D.C. They include state policy initiatives to address land use and infrastructure investment in a smart growth context as well as tax-base sharing. The report also suggests reform in federal policies and programs, including transportation investments to reinforce cities as the center of a region, fair housing enforcement, wider use of housing vouchers, and better job training and placement.

David Rusk argues that focusing only on programs directed at poor neighborhoods is a losing strategy and even the best such programs must be matched by a strong "outside game," or regional, strategy. He suggests that four policies are essential if we are to address separation by race and class, which he describes as the "toughest political issue in American society":[13]

1. Fair-share housing, encouraging low-income and moderate-income housing in all towns
2. Policies designed to ensure full access by minorities to jobs and good housing
3. Policies designed to help low-income families move into small units of scattered site housing and private rentals with rent subsidies in more balanced neighborhoods
4. Tax-sharing policies to address fiscal disparity between cities and their suburbs[14]

Myron Orfield is one of the most successful figures on the scene at achieving progress on some of these tough issues because of the tactical approach he takes. An advocate of a new "metropolitics" designed to emphasize the common interests of cities and suburbs, he is a strong proponent of both property tax equity (primarily through tax-base sharing) and shifting public infrastructure investment toward cities and first suburbs. Like others, he also advocates more housing choices for low-income and moderate-income people and addressing problems in land-use practice.

This is only a sample of the discussion and recommendations addressing decentralization and the concentration of poverty in cities. These four experts emphasize different points and disagree on some strategies, but I believe they and others would agree that we need both an inside game and an outside game, to borrow David Rusk's basketball analogy. To be sure, we must strengthen neighborhoods that low-income people live in, but mostly what we need is an outside game that connects people in poverty to opportunity throughout a region.

The Ultimate Measure of Success for Regionalism

My own experience over twenty-five years of working in the trenches in state and local government and now for a regional council of governments convinces me that this concentration of poverty and lack of access to opportunity must be addressed if we are to flourish as a nation and as a people. When

I started my career working in Trenton City Hall, I was sure we could handle all our challenges on our own. We didn't need help from any do-gooders, and we sure didn't need suburban towns looking over our shoulder. But I came to realize over time that most of our toughest problems were far beyond our reach in city hall, and that we lacked the resources and policy authority to make the kinds of change that would promote better socioeconomic balance in our city and open up access to opportunity for more city residents. Despite our best efforts, the prevailing trends made these changes more necessary and less reachable for us as time went on.

Then, while serving in state government in New Jersey, I traveled up and down the state working with local governments and community-based organizations to help low-income people move to self-sufficiency. It became quite clear, because of the growing concentration of poverty in our cities, that any long-term hope for success depended on creating stronger city-suburban linkage and opening up access to opportunity for city residents throughout a region.

I soon came to realize that cities such as Trenton and Hartford, and even larger cities such as Philadelphia, couldn't do it on their own. We need a strong outside game, one that removes barriers to opportunity for city residents and allows a better mix of income groups throughout the region. We need to deconcentrate poverty in cities and give many of the people who live in them a better shot at pursuing the American dream. Make no mistake: this will not be easy. To quote Anthony Downs, "From concentrated minority poverty comes the inner core problems that I believe are the most serious of all long-term threats to our political stability and economic prosperity."[15]

At the same time, it is by far our toughest challenge. On this point, David Rusk says that "redeeming the inner city and the urban underclass requires reintegration of city and suburb. This is the toughest political issue in American society. It goes right to the heart of America's fear about race and class. There will be no short-term, politically comfortable solutions."[16]

Downs and Rusk are right. It will be very hard to tackle this seemingly intractable problem, yet the future well-being of many regions depends on our working toward better socioeconomic balance in our communities. Without it, and without the access to opportunity that is implied, we will all eventually pay the price. Providing access to opportunity and achieving better socioeconomic balance is the ultimate measure of success in regional initiatives. It is a prerequisite for success in many of the other challenges we face, such as building a good workforce, sustaining our economic competitive edge, fighting crime, and using public tax dollars cost-effectively. Providing better access to opportunity for low-income people and especially city residents should be our overarching goal in all regional initiatives.

We should ask ourselves each time we make a decision that will affect our region and its communities, "How does this decision help or hinder us in the effort to deconcentrate poverty and open up access to opportunity?"

Many have suggested that among the major regional challenges, it might be easier to deal with congestion, open-space protection, and related smart-growth issues and to implement governance strategies designed to provide more cost-effective public services. This is because there tends to be good political support from suburban residents for these issues. But as Rusk has argued, "Regional arrangements usually avoid policies and programs that share the social burdens of inner-city residents . . . Areawide compacts on transportation planning, solid waste management, sewage treatment, and air quality management may be 'good government,' but they address the urban problem only if they attack racial and economic segregation."[17]

I agree. These good government initiatives are important and must be pursued, but they are not enough if we are honest with ourselves about our greatest challenge.

Similarly, many people, myself included, have jumped on the smart-growth bandwagon in the hope that it can be part of the answer to racial and economic segregation and the resultant lack of access to opportunity. Many of us have worked quite hard to promote proposals that fall under the smart-growth umbrella. Even so, I fear that at the end of the day, we may not have made a meaningful contribution toward achieving better socioeconomic balance in our region's communities.

In fact, some have suggested that certain smart-growth policies might actually impede creation of new affordable housing units in wealthier communities, or even reduce the supply of affordable housing in a region. The Brookings Institution and the Harvard Institute of Economic Research both looked at this question in recent publications. The Harvard study argues that an affordable housing shortage is not necessarily a problem nationwide; the price of housing is significantly higher than construction costs in only a few areas. Further, using a series of tests, this report suggests that land-use controls play a "dominant role in making housing expensive."[18] The Brookings report argues that many factors, but especially market demand, have an impact on housing prices. Smart-growth management policies can raise housing prices, but so do traditional land-use practices that have often excluded low-income people. Therefore the Brookings researchers write that the real choice is "between good and bad land use regulation to improve housing choice."[19]

As time goes on, we will get a better picture of how smart-growth policies affect the concentration of poverty in cities. I still believe that smart-growth efforts can help address the problems associated with the separation of rich and poor. But we proponents must be honest about what we hope to achieve, and we must be alert for indications that our work might not secure the hoped-for outcomes.

Conclusion

If you believe, as I do, that strengthening connections, for residents of a poor neighborhood, to opportunity throughout a region is our most important challenge, then it is important to keep your eyes on the prize. This phrase, borrowed from the civil rights era, is fitting because real progress in addressing the concentration of poverty requires a campaign of the magnitude and reach of the civil rights movement. The appeal it must make to people's sense of what is right and to people's enlightened self-interest is also similar. John Powell, the director of the Institute on Race and Poverty, says it well and succinctly: "The civil rights movement in the twenty-first century is about space."[20] He goes on to say that the way to end segregation is through regional approaches connecting people to opportunity.

We know what's needed to deconcentrate poverty: more affordable housing units in more places; stronger fair housing enforcement; better use of mobile housing vouchers; more options for K–12 education, especially for children in neighborhoods with poorly performing schools; and better access to jobs in terms of hiring practices and transportation. It is also important, in offering low-income people more housing choices, that we not create new pockets of poverty.

The flip side of this coin is that we must also build or maintain a strong middle class in our cities. We must work to make the city a place in which more middle-income families live. School options are especially important in accomplishing this.

But how can we build the broad support needed to achieve better balance in our communities and wider access to opportunity? Some of us in the Hartford region are working now to create a regional citizens network, which would address these and other regional issues. We are looking at some great models from around the country, including such places as Jacksonville, St. Louis, and Portland (Oregon). Our work in the Hartford region is in part a follow-up to a civic participation project we conducted in five towns with the help of the National Civic League. There we learned the value of strong citizen participation and informed, engaged citizenship.

It is our hope that people from all walks of life and all points of view will come together through a regional citizens network to have an honest discussion about the consequences of decentralization, and particularly the separation of rich and poor in Hartford. Then we might be ready to work together to secure the public reforms and the changes in how we live our lives that allow meaningful change in the separation of rich and poor—our most important regional challenge. Strong, hopefully broad, public support is a prerequisite for real progress in this endeavor.

Because of how we separate ourselves, many Americans are not fully aware that this separation prevents hundreds of thousands of people from making a good life and contributing to society in the process. The indirect impact on the overall well-being of a region is even less well known. I believe that most people would respond positively to this appeal if only they could see the big picture of how the concentration of poverty hurts many people and works against nearly everyone's long-term interest. The first step entails compelling, defensible information that documents trends in separation by income and the cost that this separation exacts on all of us. Myron Orfield's work (referred to earlier) in mapping out the impact of these issues can be compelling.

Then people need a forum to come together to discuss these tough issues with others from different walks of life. The goal is to arrive at a shared understanding of what serves their common interest and then to advocate together for reforms to achieve it. Some may say it is naïve to hope for this. But major changes in public attitude and public policy on tough issues have been achieved before in our nation's history. They mark points of great progress for our nation, and they represent historic events of which most Americans are justly proud. The successful civil rights movement in the 1960s is recent testimony. The critical importance of building more balanced communities and opening up access to opportunity demands we do it again. If we succeed, we will recommit our country to the fundamental principle of equality of opportunity. In the bargain, we will ensure a more prosperous and stable future for our regions and our nation.

Notes

1. Rusk, D. *Cities Without Suburbs.* Washington, D.C.: Woodrow Wilson Center Press, 1993.

2. Rusk (1993).

3. Rusk, D. *Inside Game/Outside Game: Winning Strategies for Saving Urban America.* Washington, D.C.: Brookings Institution Press, 1999.

4. Rusk (1999).

5. Gottlieb, P. D. "The Effects of Poverty on Metropolitan Area Economic Performance: A Policy Oriented Research Review." In R. Greenstein and W. Wiewel (eds.), *Urban-Suburban Interdependencies.* Cambridge, Mass.: Lincoln Institute of Land Policy, 2000.

6. Gottlieb (2000), p. 28.

7. Heffley, D. "Education ReCAPT." *Connecticut Economy (University of Connecticut Quarterly Review),* Spring 1998.

8. Benabou, R. "Workings of a City: Location, Education and Production." *Quarterly Journal of Economics,* Aug. 1993, pp. 619–652.

9. Hughes, M. A. "Poverty in Cities." (Research report.) Washington, D.C.: National League of Cities, 1989.

10. Orfield, M. *American Metropolitics.* Washington, D.C.: Brookings Institution Press, 2002.

11. Downs, A. *New Visions for Metropolitan America.* Washington, D.C., and Cambridge, Mass.: Brookings Institution and Lincoln Institute of Land Policy, 1994.

12. Katz, B. "Reviving Cities: Think Metropolitan." (Policy brief no. 33.) Washington, D.C.: Brookings Institution, June 1998.

13. Rusk (1993), p. 122.

14. Rusk (1993), p. 122.

15. Downs, A. "Some Realities About Sprawl and Urban Decline." *Housing Policy Debate* (Fannie Mae Foundation), 1999, *10*(4).

16. Rusk (1993), p. 122.

17. Rusk (1993), p. 123.

18. Glaeser, E., and Gyourko, J. *The Impact of Zoning on Housing Affordability.* Cambridge, Mass.: Harvard Institute of Economic Research, Mar. 2002.

19. Nelson, A. C., Pendall, R., Dawkins, C. J., and Knaap, G. J. *The Link Between Growth Management and Housing Affordability: The Academic Evidence.* Washington D.C.: Brookings Institute Center on Urban and Metropolitan Policy, Feb. 2002.

20. From a speech to the Greater Hartford Interfaith Coalition for Equity and Justice; comment published in the *Hartford Courant,* June 27, 2002.

Richard J. Porth is executive director of the Capitol Region Council of Governments, Hartford, Connecticut.

Leading and Learning: Multisector Collaboration Yields Civic Change and Lessons on the Nature of Progress

John H. McKoy

Over the past two decades, a trend has emerged among urban communities seeking to address the disparate needs of their rapidly diversifying citizenry. Faced with the challenges of governing an ever-transforming landscape of classes, races, nationalities, and political loyalties, some community and government leaders have embraced collaboration as a means of catalyzing change and increasing civic engagement among citizens. A mutually beneficial relationship between two or more parties, collaboration enables the partners to work toward a common goal by sharing responsibility, authority, and accountability for achieving results. Its purpose is to create a shared vision and joint strategies to address concerns that go beyond the purview of any particular party. Collaboration relies on trust, inclusion, and constructive engagement to achieve positive and enduring changes that benefit the collective good of the stakeholders. It is a system of effecting change defined by a delicate balance of institutional and organizational power. A successful collaborative endeavor requires the presence of a strong sense of community among the stakeholders.

Implementing and managing a successful collaborative project often requires the assistance of a central organization capable of forging and fostering relationships with partners in a variety of sectors. Civic intermediary organizations such as DC Agenda maintain and build relationships with leaders, individuals, and other organizations and institutions to facilitate or mobilize resources and opportunities on behalf of the underserved. They facilitate discussion with stakeholders—from neighborhood leaders to elected officials—in developing a common understanding of some of the problems facing a community. They are often positioned in such a way as to enable bridging race and class differences. They often work to strengthen a community by working behind the scenes to enhance the leadership capacity of community-based organizations and institutions such as schools, social service providers, and neighborhood organizations. In many cases, a civic intermediary organization is also influential in using connections with funding institutions to broker resources for a financially disadvantaged community.

Managing Collaborative Endeavors:
DC Agenda as Community Builder

DC Agenda is one such civic intermediary organization. It was founded in 1994 by the Federal City Council, a prestigious business association responsible for promoting numerous public projects in Washington, D.C. Its primary goal is to identify the challenges, and support the opportunities, facing the District of Columbia. Although begun under the auspices of the Federal City Council, it has since grown into a distinct 501(c)(3) nonprofit organization, with an annual operating budget of $1.6 million and a staff of fourteen dedicated professionals.

Although the growth of DC Agenda from a project to an independent corporation attests to success at forging civic improvement, the atmosphere in which it operates has changed drastically since inception. At the time of DC Agenda's founding, Washington, D.C., was in fiscal disarray. Businesses and middle-class residents were leaving, city services were mismanaged, and the quality of the city's public schools was declining. The situation was further worsened by a complex interplay of race and class issues, and the historically flawed relations between the U.S. Congress and the district government. Congress forbids the district from taxing commuters who work in DC (a group that comprises approximately two-thirds of the workforce); has removed many large organizations, such as the World Bank and Fannie Mae from the city's tax roles; and can veto any city budget proposal or legislation. Washington, D.C., has many of the budgetary expenditures of a city, a county, and a state, yet it has less authority—notably, lack of voting representation in Congress. The severity of the city's fiscal and sociopolitical problems was further intensified by the failure of successive municipal administrations to address effectively the pressing policy and management challenges confronting the city.

DC Agenda was formed as a new and innovative way to address the fiscal, political, social, and economic crises of the District of Columbia. Given the fragmentation of power in the city at that time, it was clear that no single group's actions would be sufficient to move the city in a new direction. Meaningful change would only come if all interested groups were engaged in the reform process. Furthermore, new forms of collaboration would be required between the district government and the Congress and federal government; between the public and private sectors; and among the diverse racial, economic, and ethnic groups residing in the city. In addition, current and accurate information, clear analysis, and new strategies would be needed to guide and support the required levels of collaboration. An independent community assistance organization committed to community building principles was required to fill these roles.

Since its inception, DC Agenda has employed cross-sector collaboration as a successful means of addressing the fiscal, social, and economic problems that plague the District of Columbia. Acting in partnership with existing organizations and institutions, it aims to strengthen the community bonds and personal networks that give rise to effective civic involvement. It helps generate and leverage resources, influence local policy, expand civic infrastructure, and build bridges across sectors.

DC Agenda arrived at its current role having evolved through three phases: situation analysis, civic participation process, and implementation. Its progress through these phases illustrates an effective framework for community change.

In 1994, the DC Agenda Project was initiated by the Federal City Council with phase one, a situation analysis. Studies were solicited from the Greater Washington Research Center, McKinsey and Co., the Urban Institute, and the Wirthlin Group to establish a common base of current and accurate information regarding the conditions related to the city's intensifying crisis. These studies examined the migration patterns into and out of the city; the causes of, and potential remedies to, Washington's fiscal and economic crisis; and the attitudes of district and suburban residents regarding the city, its problems, and its prospects.

The following year, phase two, the civic participation process, was launched. The DC Agenda Project organized broad civic discussion with key stakeholders to identify a feasible set of strategic priorities around which consensus could be developed for improving the city. The outcomes of a series of focus groups led to recommendations for action in six critical areas: fiscal and governance; economic development; youth, families, and neighborhoods; public education; public safety; and health.

As phase two drew to a close, it became clear that backup assistance was needed as stakeholders sought to implement these recommendations. In 1995, the DC Agenda Support Corporation was formed as an independent nonprofit entity to support phase three, an ongoing implementation process. Today, DC Agenda's core activities and programs continue to support implementation of identified priorities. Three of the major initiatives supported by DC Agenda, discussed in this article, are examples of successfully using collaboration to involve community and government stakeholders in accomplishing impressive results.

The relationships that DC Agenda built throughout the city during phase one and phase two and the staff it hired placed the organization in a unique situation, to take on many of the capacity-building functions that were identified by its own initial studies. DC Agenda's involvement with the Children and Youth Investment Partnership (CYIP) and the National Capital Revitalization Corporation (NCRC) emerged from partnerships that DC Agenda had built with stakeholders while researching topics and coordinating planning activities that led to proposals for those organizations. After codifying which issues needed to be addressed to strengthen communities and neighborhoods so as to facilitate the city's overall economic recovery, DC Agenda specified six focus areas for future attention:

1. Fiscal and governance
2. Economic development
3. Public education
4. Public safety
5. Health
6. Children, youth, families, and neighborhoods

DC Agenda's involvement with the Healthy Families/Thriving Communities Collaboratives, however, evolved through a different process. In 1995, Jerome Miller, who was then the court-appointed receiver of the city's Child and Family Services Agency, asked DC Agenda to act as fiscal agent for the city's burgeoning neighborhood social service collaboratives. As DC Agenda's relationship with the collaboratives deepened, other services were identified and procured, such as management consulting and capacity-building technical assistance.

The Healthy Families/Thriving Communities Collaboratives

The Healthy Families/Thriving Communities (HFTC) Collaboratives have helped to dramatically expand and strengthen services available to youths and families in the District of Columbia.

The HFTC Collaboratives are a network of nonprofit service providers, civic and resident associations, faith communities, community leaders, and involved citizens working together to prevent child abuse and neglect in the city's most at-risk neighborhoods. Based on the premise that child welfare agencies are often too isolated from the communities they serve, the HFTC Collaboratives were created in 1993 when public and private advocates recommended a neighborhood-based approach to solving the child abuse and neglect problems that plagued many of the city's poorest neighborhoods.

In 1994, the District of Columbia's child welfare system was placed in receivership under the auspices of the Child and Family Services Agency. CFSA was responsible for improving the system's management, infrastructure, staffing, training, quality assurance, and resource development. The city was also required by the consent decree governing the receivership to decentralize the child welfare system and work with community leaders in reconstructing an effective system of service delivery. Miller embraced the HFTC Collaboratives as the framework through which the city could begin providing neighborhood-based child and family support services. To support development of the collaboratives, DC Agenda was asked to serve as the technical services provider and logistical coordinator to the collaboratives. Today, there are seven HFTC Collaboratives operating in the District of Columbia. In 2000, some thirteen hundred families, including thirty-six hundred children, received services through the collaboratives.

The collaboratives work in partnership with CFSA to provide services to families involved with the child protection system or at risk of becoming involved in the system. They offer case management services to families and children who are community referrals; families facing difficulty but not involved with CFSA; and families having open protective service cases. The collaboratives also operate family support centers, where individuals, families, and youths can receive referral to other services, participate in activities or programs, and learn new skills. The centers also host support groups to discuss teen health and mentoring, substance abuse and prevention, and domestic violence.

The HFTC collaboratives work with CFSA on the structure of the service delivery system, offer training for collaborative staff members, contribute to development of practice standards, and play a key role in implementing and supporting family case conferencing. They also work with such other city agencies as the Department of Mental Health, the public schools, and the Department of Housing to make other critical supports available as needed.

From 1996 to 2001, DC Agenda served as fiscal intermediary for the HFTC Collaboratives, accepting federal agency reimbursement on their behalf and providing capacity-building assistance to each neighborhood-level group. In 2001, DC Agenda helped establish the citywide Collaborative Council as an independent body that oversees programmatic, fiscal, and administrative development of Washington's seven neighborhood collaboratives. The council helps ensure standard practices and quality services throughout the neighborhood network.

The city's original paradigm of family support services failed, as it was impossible for a single, highly centralized agency to effectively address the spectrum of need among families with multiple problems throughout the diverse neighborhoods of the city. The HFTC Collaboratives are successful because they connect a needy family with an array of collaborating services that normally function independently of one another. By connecting services and bringing them closer to the client, the collaboratives extend support to a family before problems begin to develop, helping to prevent the family's becoming lost in city bureaucracy.

The Children Youth Investment Partnership

Another successful example of DC Agenda's work to forge multisector collaboration is the Children and Youth Investment Partnership. CYIP was formed to respond to a crisis condition of duplicative, sometimes ineffective, and usually uncoordinated out-of-school time services for the district's young people. Many key outcomes for the city's children and youths were unacceptably below national norms: Scholastic Aptitude Test scores in the city were two hundred points below the national score average; 18 percent of all births in the city were to teenage mothers; and the death rate among teens age fifteen to nineteen was almost three times the national average.

In 1995, some three hundred neighborhood and civic leaders convened to explore issues relating to neighborhood revitalization, crime prevention, and public safety. They focused on the absence of integrated out-of-school-time services tailored to the needs of the city's children and youth. Out of this meeting, the D.C. Forum for Collaboration and Support was born. The forum, which consisted of members of individuals and organizations that provide youth services, began, with the assistance of DC Agenda, to explore ways of improving the city's programs for children and youth. A series of discussions between January 1998 and June 1999 rallied parents, youths, service providers, government agencies, and members of the private sector to develop a citywide youth investment strategy, and CYIP was born.

Today, CYIP represents a triumph in multisector collaboration. Although the primary goal of the partnership is to coordinate out-of-school-time programs for children and youth, it also serves to facilitate collaboration and communication among members of the public and private sectors. The partnership is composed of civic organizations and nonprofits, among them DC Agenda; city government agencies, such as the Office of the Deputy Mayor for Children, Youth, and Families; the Office of Early Childhood Development; the public schools; the district's employment services department; the parks and recreation department; and the public library. Other partners in CYIP include the Urban Institute and community-based organizations such as the HFTC Collaboratives.

With support from city government, DC Agenda took the lead in chartering the Children Youth Investment Trust Corporation (CYITC). It also raised private resources to fund its startup activities. CYITC is responsible for coordinating the activities of the partnership by convening and fostering communication among, and allocating funding to, stakeholders. CYITC also mobilizes public support for the partnership. In 2000, the City Council, at the mayor's urging, allocated $12 million to the corporation, which began distributing those funds to CYIP's out-of-school-time and entrepreneurship programs for youth. Subsequent allocations from the city have brought the total of city government support extended to the corporation to $22 million.

CYITC functions as logistical coordinator and fiscal manager for this collaboration; the D.C. Public Schools Aftercare Program constitutes a significant portion of the services provided by the partnership. The program makes out-of-school-time academic and nonacademic activities (such as arts, recreation, health, and community service) available to elementary and middle school students throughout the city. It receives funding from Temporary Aid for Needy Families (TANF) and the federal Department of Education, and it represents the partnership's efforts to offer comprehensive out-of-school-time programming to children and youth through use of the DCPS's institutional resources. Some twenty thousand additional children in the city have participated in after-school programs since the partnership was formed in 1999.

Using expertise in facilitation, as well as data collection, research, and evaluation activities, CYIP develops and shares resources among multiple partners that otherwise would not have had the opportunity or resources to work together.

The National Capital Revitalization Corporation

Also exemplary of DC Agenda's effectiveness as a community intermediary is creation of the National Capital Revitalization Corporation (NCRC). NCRC is a publicly chartered real estate company that convenes public and private partners to implement large-scale real estate projects to strengthen the district's economic base. The goal of the corporation is to spur economic development in Washington, D.C., especially in at-risk neighborhoods. As with the HFTC Collaboratives and CYIP, cross-sector collaboration played an important role in forming NCRC.

Spearheaded by DC Agenda through a demanding three-year process, NCRC was created by representatives of the municipal and federal governments and the private sector, and officially born with passage of the National Capital Revitalization Corporation Act of 1998. NCRC was the brainchild of city council representative Charlene Drew Jarvis (who was then a DC Agenda board member). It supports large-scale commercial development projects intended to expand both the employment base for D.C. residents and the city's own tax base by leveraging public and private resources and expertise. Its guiding vision is that this will be achieved by bringing nonprofit economic and commercial development organizations together with the federal and city governments to finance and facilitate projects to stimulate investment in D.C. neighborhoods.

Once the 1998 act passed, Congress approved $25 million in federal seed money for development of the NCRC. These funds were held by the federal treasury department for NCRC's start up, earmarked for project development, capital investments, loans, and administrative purposes. Fannie Mae, the city's largest business corporation, pledged an additional $75 million. DC Agenda's economic development committee (composed of stakeholders from the federal government, the city government, local neighborhood-based economic groups, and corporations) served as a steering body for the NCRC, recruiting candidates for its board of directors and advising the mayor on executive issues related to NCRC's startup activities.

As with other collaborations, partnerships played an important role in creating the NCRC. It was, and continues to be, regarded as a vital institution to support the city's economic resurgence by linking the expertise and resources of stakeholders from diverse leadership sectors. From its inception, the corporation has been envisioned as a powerful and flexible private-public economic development entity capable of achieving results that individual elements of the partnership have been unable to accomplish alone. Its creation and operations alike reflect a carefully forged collaboration between the district government, the federal government, and the private sector. DC Agenda's economic development committee was instrumental in galvanizing public support of the NCRC and obtaining federal funding for the project.

Today, the NCRC is the city's chief economic development authority. It promotes and capitalizes on economic development opportunities by providing guidance, capital, land, marketing, packaging, and coordination services for commercial and mixed-use real estate development projects. It has quickly become a proactive force facilitating economic growth in Washington neighborhoods, helping to change previous perceptions of the city as a tough place to do business. Its use of resources from a spectrum of public and private sources works because it yields leadership and expertise while maintaining a smooth relationship with appropriate city agencies.

Although it is too soon to measure the long-term impact on economic and commercial development in Washington, in the year since incorporation NCRC has made tremendous progress in revitalizing abandoned and unused parcels of land throughout the city. NCRC currently has four major projects under way, notably plans to develop mixed-use retail, residential, and artists' space in the Mount Vernon Square area of the city as well as plans to revitalize the waterfront area of southwest Washington to increase the presence of retail and entertainment facilities, and to link the area to the National Mall and the city's other major tourist attractions.

How Collaborations Are Making a Difference

Recent improvements in the city's civic life demonstrate DC Agenda's success at fostering collaborative partnerships. The HFTC Collaboratives have created a network of community-based service providers that work together efficiently and effectively as a web of support for at-risk families and neighborhoods. The collaboratives have formed a citywide collaborative council, a governing body consisting of representatives from each neighborhood collaborative. The council oversees and assists the collaboratives with standard setting, strategic planning, and evaluation. With formation of the Collaborative Council, individual collaboratives now work together more efficiently, and measures have been set in place to qualify and quantify the effectiveness of the services provided by the collaboratives. Although it is too soon to determine the long-term impact of the Collaborative Council, there should be an improvement of child and family services among neighborhood service providers.

As a result of the efforts made by CYIP, thousands more children and youths throughout the District of Columbia receive out-of-school-time educational services, thus enhancing their school performance and ensuring that more kids have educational and career opportunities beyond high school. Since NCRC's launch, long-dormant city owned parcels have been sold and are being renovated by neighborhood community development corporations and for profit developers, stimulating economic growth and also seeking solutions to the displacement often caused by gentrification.

The Collaborative Process

To ensure a successful collaborative endeavor, steps must be taken to create the optimum balance of interests and power among stakeholders. Each of them comes to the table with its own resources, but generally speaking they all share a similar commitment to problem solving. Like many practitioners of collaboration, DC Agenda views the process as occurring in phases. Creation and implementation of the initiatives described in this article followed steps that tend to be common in a collaborative endeavor: an initiation phase, an action-planning phase, and an implementation phase.

Before any of these projects could begin, a steering group of interested stakeholders convened to examine the situation and clearly define the pertinent issues. This assessment identified the issues that the partnership hoped to address as well as the needs, vision, and potential outcomes associated with the project. In this phase, participants sought to involve additional stakeholders and promote support for the project to ensure a more inclusive and democratic vision.

With the convening of the appropriate stakeholders and clear definition of the project vision and outcomes, the collaborative process was established. In this second phase, stakeholders establish ground rules for working together. They rigorously define and analyze the problems inherent in the project, identify alternate strategies and solutions, and commit to clear and achievable results. This phase concludes with creation of an action plan.

In phase three, participants concentrate on facilitating implementation of the action plan. This usually entails identifying or creating an administrative entity to coordinate logistics and provide ongoing technical assistance to the project. Once the implementation is under way, participants work with staff and consultants to monitor, manage, build external support for, and document the progress of the initiative.

Implementation, by definition, begins to produce outcomes. Participants focus on assessing the progress of the project, drawing lessons from successes and mistakes. They continue working to expand stakeholder investment and build the external supports necessary to sustain the initiative.

What These Experiences Have Taught Us About Collaboration

Creating partnership among diverse stakeholders is not without complication. In fact, collaborations involving nonprofit, community, corporate, and government partners reveal valuable lessons regarding the nature of civic progress:

- Each collaboration involves unique processes and yields unique results.
- Convening parties must identify and form strategic collaborative partnerships.
- Stakeholder interests must be identified and addressed.
- Stakeholders must feel important to the process.
- Small victories should be declared and celebrated along the way.
- Stakeholders, not staff, must be allowed to guide the collaborative process.
- Conveners of the collaboration should encourage offline communication, and communication between subgroups of stakeholders; few binding decisions are reached in big meetings, and power holders resist infatuation with process.
- Collaboration succeeds by forging relationships with policy makers.
- Practitioners of collaboration must stay focused on outcomes.

Even though certain sets of actions are common to collaborative processes, it is important to emphasize that there is no clear road map to coordinating partnership among diverse stakeholders. Indeed, most collaborative endeavors are specific to the particular context in which they arise. What works in one city, or for a certain issue, may not work for another place or in other circumstances. Thus, participants in a complex collaborative endeavor must remain flexible and be willing and able to adapt to myriad unforeseen challenges.

Securing the sustained involvement of relevant partners has been the key to success for the HFTC Collaboratives, CYIP, and the NCRC. This has included recruiting the appropriate partners for each project, determining the right time to include them, and working to balance the interests of partners with the interests of the project. It is also essential that stakeholders remain engaged. Any successful collaboration requires the participation of all relevant stakeholders.

To ensure their continued participation, stakeholders must experience progress or small victories in having an impact on the problems at hand. Every participant must feel like a vital component of the collaborative process and sense that the collaboration is steered by the input of each participant. Because one phase or aspect of the collaborative process may be more relevant to certain stakeholders than others, some communication may take place between subgroups of participants. This requires knowing when to involve whoever is essential to running an effective collaborative endeavor; trying to force participation at every stage may prove counterproductive.

Much of the work executed in the examples described in this article took place in small meetings, on the phone, or by e-mail. Subcommittees composed of those partners who were truly interested in, or capable of, moving an issue forward proved crucial to the collaborative process. Making progress on an issue often depended on introducing new ideas, such as those presented by a staff member or consultant. Some ideas required exploration, organization, and evaluation by an individual outside the cauldron of stakeholder group dynamics.

DC Agenda's working relationships with political and policy-making institutions in the city were critical to the success of the collaborations described in this article. Engaging government leaders (municipal and federal) and corporate associations did more than lend credence to these initiatives; relationships of this sort boosted the projects' visibility and access to resources and ultimately led to their success. Including political leaders in the collaborative process also helps to produce more of a long-term payoff. Smaller stakeholders with low visibility are able to participate in the political arena, and all participants are exposed to differing approaches to influencing the policy-making process.

Finally, it is essential to remember that although meetings, focus groups, and telephone calls and e-mails may guide the collaboration, these communications are only means to the desired end. Staff, consultants, and stakeholders who become too enamored of group technique and process or the technology of communication may lose the interest of key participants who are engaged solely to solve a problem affecting them. Steering the project toward specific results can help prevent participants from becoming bogged down in the details of the collaborative process and will ultimately create successful outcomes.

Continuing Collaboration

Our experience with facilitating multisector exchanges has taught us that collaborative partnership can address enormously complex problems and create lasting and effective change. Yet as government performance improves and community economic conditions change, the issues that the civic intermediary addresses also change. To remain relevant, intermediaries must change with the times, providing new services and expertise to reflect the shifting sociopolitical context within which they work.

Often, an intermediary organization may determine that particular resources and expertise are better suited to address a more specific or localized problem than it initially set forth to concentrate on. This trend is particularly prevalent after the intermediary has successfully created a network of partners to solve a particular problem. In many cases, that network becomes capable of addressing an issue more effectively than the intermediary. When this occurs, the intermediary can close up shop or identify new issues on which to focus.

In other cases, an intermediary may decide that rather than changing the focal issues, it may instead be more beneficial to alter how the organization seeks to effect change. In such cases, the civic intermediary may revise its strategic focus and develop new approaches to problem solving.

The Urban Strategies Council, a civic intermediary based in Oakland, California, is an excellent example of this latter phenomenon. It began as an organization using its analytical and networking capacity to lobby for a dedicated youth investment fund from the city's annual general fund budget. After achieving this goal, subsequent reevaluation of the council's priorities and expertise led to a shift in focus to supporting neighborhood transformation. The council redefined the strategic focus to concentrate on building community capacity to conduct analysis and lobby for change on its own behalf.

As conditions in the District of Columbia improved for businesses and residents, DC Agenda's role in the community has changed to reflect shifting social and economic priorities. Demand for the convening, research, and capacity-building services of a community-building intermediary continue to exist even though the particular crises that DC Agenda's early initiatives were created to address are no longer present.

Pursuant to its recently updated strategic plan, DC Agenda continues to convene and facilitate partnerships among stakeholders and to serve as a technical assistance provider to new initiatives. Reflecting input from a broad survey involving partners from numerous sectors and civic stakeholders across the city, DC Agenda continues to focus on strengthening the community's civic infrastructure by supporting balanced neighborhood growth and youth development.

DC Agenda recently launched an equitable development initiative to respond to some of the adverse social and economic consequences that accompany neighborhood revitalization. Equitable development seeks to promote creation and maintenance of an economically and socially diverse community. This goal is pursued through policies that enhance the opportunity for lower-income residents to become homeowners, business owners, and active community participants.

DC Agenda will explore such tools and techniques as loans and grants to residents of neighborhoods threatened by gentrification. It examines the potential uses of asset creation resources such as tenant ownership of apartments, resident ownership of community businesses, and job training. DC Agenda's equitable development initiative also builds community by strengthening networks among citizens. These networks empower residents of underserved neighborhoods by helping them to better identify and solve neighborhood issues, link them to government policy makers, and connect them with jobs and job training opportunities.

DC Agenda's Center for Neighborhood Information Services (NIS) will play a central role in these activities. NIS produces current and reliable data and analysis about neighborhoods throughout the city. This information is intended to facilitate the strategic decision-making processes of government and community organizations.

NIS will use its data collection capabilities to produce an issue scan, identifying indicators of community health in D.C. neighborhoods. The issue scan will be produced in partnership with research organizations such as the Brookings Institution, the Urban Institute, and local universities. It is to be published annually and used in conjunction with neighborhood-based focus groups to determine the issues that demand the immediate attention of city government as well as those issues that lend themselves to collaborative solution.

NIS will also play a major role in DC Agenda's Neighborhood Support Program (NSP), a new initiative for building capacity among leaders at the neighborhood level. This program, designed in partnership with organizations including the University of the District of Columbia (UDC) and the city's Humanities Council, seeks to improve the ability of neighborhood leaders to be more effective players in creating successful and sustainable communities. One of the modules in a curriculum designed for neighborhood leaders will help them understand how to use data collection and analysis techniques to describe neighborhood conditions.

Another DC Agenda initiative, the Collaborative Leadership Laboratory, will bring together players from the government, private, and nonprofit sectors to help leadership acquire new problem-solving and change management skills. The CLL fosters a safe learning environment where leaders can consider different approaches to regional problem solving, such as when mediation is appropriate and when leaders should rely on negotiation. CLL also helps leaders decide when and how to create environments and frameworks that employ a collaborative approach and how to build a network of experts and community leaders trained in the intricacies of cross-sector collaboration.

DC Agenda's successful involvement with applying the collaborative process has worked well for Washington, D.C., in addressing a variety of issues. DC Agenda continues to help the city's leaders improve critical outcomes for residents by applying the learning from past triumphs to future endeavors. By connecting civic leaders to key issues, exploiting a network of key partners, and offering convening skills and capacity-building expertise, DC Agenda forges new and sustained solutions to urban challenges.

Civic issues and priorities change over time, but addressing the city's challenges and needs in the future continues to require approaches that connect civic leaders to each other around current and accurate information. These networks and partnerships create a whole that is greater than the sum of its participants. DC Agenda will be there, helping to lead, learn, and serve, by offering convening skills and capacity-building expertise and resources as a champion of civic change through collaboration.

John H. McKoy is president and CEO of DC Agenda, Washington, D.C.

If You Only Knew How Well We Are Performing, You'd Be Highly Satisfied with the Quality of Our Service

Janet M. Kelly

Sixty-two years ago, the political scientist V. O. Key articulated the indictment that still plagues public finance: public budgeting has no theory. Specifically, Key asked, "On what basis shall it be decided to allocate X dollars to activity A instead of activity B?"[1] We may finally be getting our answer to Key's question in the form of an emerging budgetary theory, but many public finance professionals are not comfortable with it. This emerging theory comes from a commendable effort to make government more accountable to citizens, and it rests on the assumption that citizens hold the same definition of accountability as the one being advocated by the reform proponents. A reformed or "reinvented" government, in this perspective, seeks to be accountable for results, defining a result as an aspect of service provision that lends itself to measurement and accountability as accurately reporting how well the government scored on it.

Public finance professionals are worried about two aspects of the reform movement. The first is whether what citizens want from their government can be counted. The second goes back to the budgetary theory. Governments prioritize what they measure. The act of measuring an activity ensures that resources are directed toward achieving the performance target set for it. So we have our answer to Key's question about the basis on which dollars are allocated to activity A instead of activity B: if we measure the performance of activity A and not that of activity B, then resources go to A. Citizen participation initiatives of the last three decades were intended to help leaders decide between A and B, sometimes by formalizing a structure for citizen input to the budget process. The new "accountability for results" movement in public management may have just the opposite effect on citizen participation.

The Roots of Reform

The philosophy behind the new accountability movement is a restatement of the reform tradition of the Progressive Era. Recall that reformers believed the political machine undermined efficient and effective governance, and they asserted that the sublimation of politics by administrative decision rules based on management science would enhance realization of the public interest. As in the Progressive Era, the contemporary reform movement emerged during a period in American history when confidence in government was low but confidence in the private sector was high. Although there is no consensus definition, in general the accountability movement involves application of private sector values to public activity. The emphasis on outcomes and not process (the latter being associated with unreformed public management) gives a priority to identifying the goals of a department or agency and measuring progress toward them. The commitment to the public interest of both the reformers of a hundred years ago and those of today is not disputed. Rather, the point of this article is to note that the methods of the new accountability movement may, in the name of reform, limit the responsiveness of government services to citizen preference.

By the early 1990s, professional organizations for public managers had begun to define accountability as performance (see, for example, the resolutions and position papers from the American Society for Public Administration [ASPA], the International City/County Management Association [ICMA], and the Government Finance Officers Association [GFOA]). The difficulty with their advocacy position on performance measurements was that the link between good performance on a set of selected indicators and increased citizen satisfaction with the services from the high-performing departments was assumed but not demonstrated. If accountability equals performance, then an outcome is defined as attainment of a performance goal. The means and ends are identical. By and large, public administration scholars have been silent on the matter, perhaps because they did not want to be associated with the old public management, where commitment to process is now regarded as a way of avoiding being accountable for results. It is interesting that my fellow bean counters are on the front lines of dissent, asserting that government must fashion its priorities and then measure the results, not the reverse.

Measuring Government Performance

The tool of the new accountability movement is performance measurement. It has been widely adopted in local government as evidence of administrative professionalism, at the urging of public professional organizations. Many observers believe performance indicators are helpful to department managers, who use them to monitor service input and output. They also routinely appear in the annual budget document, though deliberation about which department gets what is rarely based on performance standards. Local government often involves citizens in service planning and delivery decisions that may or may not be captured by these performance measures. A change may be coming that could induce local government to weigh responsiveness to citizen preferences for service against "good numbers" in the performance standards. The Governmental Accounting Standards Board (GASB) may require performance reporting in state and local government annual financial reports beginning in 2004. If so, performance measures can be audited, just like every other entry in the government's annual financial report.

So, how is it that mandatory performance reporting as a means toward GASB's stated goal of making government more accountable to citizens might actually diminish government responsiveness to citizen preference? The answer is that external auditing of the performance measures directs or redirects resources to the activity being measured. Whether the activity measured is consistent with citizen preference is an open question. The GASB has not yet determined if all governments will be required to measure the same aspects of service performance, or if governments will be allowed to select their own performance measures.

The problem with standardized measures is obvious. There is no such thing as a typical local government. Differences in income, race, ethnicity, size, geographic location, and other factors make "one size fits all" performance measures unworkable. However, if a local government can choose its own measures, perhaps with citizen input, the external auditor will verify that the performance report is accurate. But citizens and governments can only choose aspects of service performance that are measurable, and there is no evidence that citizens prioritize service indicators that can be counted. In fact, for some services (such as police), citizens may place a high priority on responsiveness to problems peculiar to their neighborhood. Typical citywide measures of police performance—number of arrests, response time, clearance rate, per capita moving violations—are poor proxies for this complicated construct.

Even the most ardent supporters of performance measurement as a tool of government accountability acknowledge the limitations of a proxy measure of service outcomes. That is why service inputs and outputs are much more commonly measured than service outcomes. Yet there is no evidence that citizens care how many officers the city has, nor how many moving violations those officers issued in the previous year. To bridge the gap between what is measured and what is valued, reform proponents have asserted that the act of measuring and reporting itself constitutes accountability to citizens, and that citizens would be more satisfied with the quality of their services if they knew how well their service providers were performing. That is, accountability to citizens means maximizing a proxy measure of service quality under the assumption that disparity in performance and citizen satisfaction with services is the result of an information problem (hence this article's title). Therefore, it is not necessary to actually involve citizens in service decisions—or even learn their preference—to be accountable to them for results.

Circular Reasoning About Citizen Satisfaction

Well, why not just measure citizen satisfaction with service performance, work toward improving satisfaction, and let the auditors verify that the survey was done properly? The GASB recently completed a report on citizens' attitude and experience with performance measures. Drawn from focus group discussion with citizens invited by their government (nine cities, two counties, four states) to participate, GASB concluded that citizens should be involved in selecting performance measures and determining how results should be disseminated. They affirmed that outcome data are more important than input or output but only briefly mentioned the customer satisfaction survey as the one source of outcome data that reflects citizen priorities and preferences. The GASB, like most other organizations committed to reform through performance measurement, is far more comfortable with the citizen as recipient of performance information than with the citizen as provider of performance information. Below the surface statement that the citizen can be a valuable source of service information lies a conviction that the average citizen just doesn't know enough about his or her services and service providers to offer anything of value to the committed reformer.

Imagine the private sector asserting that its customers just don't have enough information to make a good decision about satisfaction with a product, and that a more "reliable" measure of product quality should be substituted for the user's assessment. Government need not alter its products to reflect customer preference, so long as the internal measures of service performance reveal a high-quality product is being delivered. If citizens are not satisfied with the product, they need to be educated about the achieved quality standards. In other words, government must advertise how accountable it is to citizens for giving them what they should want. Citizens can hold their government accountable, though on the government's terms, not their own. If the reformed, reinvented public agency is flexible and adaptive to citizen/customer demands, why are citizens expected to do all the adapting?

What We Don't Know About Performance and Citizen Satisfaction

The academic and professional community could just accept that high performance is, or ought to be, associated with citizen satisfaction. Fortunately, we are still in the business of testing assumptions, even when the rhetoric gets tough (nobody wants to be labeled "antireform"). The relationship between service performance and citizen satisfaction is not an easy one to test. There are serious issues in operationalizing service productivity and citizen satisfaction that limit confidence in results. Still, we've overcome greater barriers when an important issue was at stake.

I recently regressed common input, output, and outcome performance measures in four service areas (police, fire, roads, and parks) on citizen satisfaction scores for those services in fifty-three cities. The cities were a nonrandom subset of participants in a performance benchmarking study sponsored by GASB and the ICMA, with a grant from the Alfred P. Sloan foundation. There was no relationship between the standardized citywide service satisfaction score for the four service areas and the standardized service performance score. Satisfaction was not related to input measures such as total service budget or number of park employees, output measures such as police response time, or outcome measures such as the percentage of road miles assessed as being in good condition. Moreover, aggregate satisfaction was not related to race, income, or education level. These preliminary conclusions need to be confirmed by another study with randomly selected jurisdictions, which would allow the research to move beyond the relatively few participants in the GASB/ICMA/Sloan project. However, the expected result did not obtain, nor has any other research established it.

Governments Do What They Measure

Just as there are few unobtrusive measures in the social sciences, there are no unobtrusive measures of performance in public management. What is measured affects what is done. Moreover, managers measure what they value, so performance measurement becomes a value-defining exercise as well. If efficiency is measured, the organization seeks it. If outputs are measured, they become evidence of good performance. Performance measures don't just describe what public organizations do; they reveal what managers think they *should* do. If managers shape those definitions, then the performance measurement process reflects managerial values. Managerial values may be a reasonable and appropriate reform goal, but we must scruple to acknowledge that our actions and our rhetoric are not perfectly consistent (unless one assumes that managerial goals reflect citizen preference). As practiced, we assert that managerial values are what citizens *should* prefer.

This may be less hubris than practical necessity on the part of managers. When a public organization engages in performance measurement to promote accountability, it invariably measures the means used to achieve a goal rather than the goal itself. Goals are frightfully hard to quantify in the public sector. There may be multiple simultaneous goals, some of which compete with one another. Goals may change with the political environment or public opinion. Means are much more stable and easier to quantify, making them the logical alternative. Means often suggest the goal and measure the progress the agency makes toward it. However, means are not goals, and the difference is more than trivial. Hence the assumption of citizen/customer accountability actually requires two steps. First, the goals selected must reflect citizen/customer preference, and second, the means must be an appropriate proxy for those goals. The prospect of an external audit of the means would likely institutionalize them without necessarily aligning them with goals or preferences.

The Governmental Accounting Standards Board

The GASB was formed in 1984 by agreement of the Financial Accounting Foundation; the American Institute of Certified Public Accountants; the Government Finance Officers Association; the National Association of State Auditors, Comptrollers and Treasurers; and the seven organizations representing state and local government officials. These entities demanded one clear set of standards for governmental accounting and financial reporting that would apply to all governments and governmental entities (including universities). The GASB is governed by a five-member board drawn from member organizations; it has a small permanent staff and is funded by institutional, corporate, and individual memberships.

When the GASB is considering a new standard, an *exposure draft* is issued, signaling that members are deliberating upon a statement that will affect current standards. The next step is a *concepts statement,* where governments are encouraged to voluntarily comply with the standard. The final step is a *statement,* which establishes the standard. Compliance with GASB statements is mandatory and written into many state laws and local ordinances.

In 1994 the GASB issued concept statement number two, on service efforts and accomplishments (SEA) reporting, establishing the link between government performance and financial reporting: "Since the purpose of financial reporting is to provide information to users of financial information, the information most useful to users would be how well the government in question is performing."[2] The statement went on to describe how the proposed standards constituted accountability to citizens for government performance: "Because the primary purpose of governmental entities is to maintain or improve the well-being of their citizens, information that will assist users in assessing how efficiently and effectively governmental entities are using resources to maintain or improve the well-being of their citizens should play an important role in [financial reporting]."[3]

SEA reporting involves measures of service accomplishment (output and outcome indicators) and measures that relate service efforts to service accomplishment (efficiency and cost-outcome indicators). Rather than require SEA reporting immediately, the GASB chose to study performance reporting to determine if SEAs could be developed that meet certain criteria: relevance, understandability, comparability, timeliness, consistency, and reliability. That study is still being done (with the cooperation of the Sloan Foundation and the ICMA). GASB declined to issue a statement at the end of the first study period in 2000, choosing instead to extend the study period through 2003. In the interim, most cities began to incorporate SEA reporting in their financial statements. The SEA data are not subject to audit, because GASB has not issued a statement. If (some say *when*) GASB issues their statement in 2004, the SEAs will be subject to audit.

In anticipation of a debate on the audit basis, some commentators on an SEA reporting requirement have asserted that no performance measure can ever satisfy the criteria by which GASB would evaluate them.[4] Others suggest that public managers' resistance to SEA reporting standards indicates that they do not want to be held accountable for the programs they manage.[5] Indeed, the most vocal opposition to mandatory SEA reporting comes from none other than the professional organization of government financial managers. In a strongly worded policy statement, the GFOA accused GASB of reaching far beyond its competency in accounting and financial reporting to set standards for the quality of public services.[6] A recent policy statement was even more blunt. Consider these three excerpts:

• The GFOA emphatically rejects GASB's attempt to assert its own self-imposed and ill-defined concept of "accountability" to justify the extension of its jurisdiction to virtually all aspects of public finance.

In the public sector, goals and objectives are the concrete realization and reflection of public policy. In a democracy, it is the unique prerogative of elected and appointed officials to set public policy. If GASB were to mandate reporting of specific performance measures, it would be effectively usurping this prerogative.

• There is no such thing as a "neutral" performance measure. The selection of what to measure inevitably drives performance. Therefore, it is unrealistic to believe that performance measures mandated by GASB will remain purely informational and somehow not have an effect on how governments manage their programs.[7]

• If the counting determines the doing, then how will things be different? And what becomes of the established venues for citizen participation in service delivery decisions when those decisions are externally audited, if not externally determined?

Implications for Public Managers and Citizens

Not all service decisions can and should involve citizen participation. In general, decisions that require a great degree of quality should not involve the public, while decisions that require a great degree of acceptability can benefit from public involvement.[8] In the case of a decision that requires both quality and acceptability, tension is expected if citizens' preferences do not align with bureaucratic decision rules. Service decisions may fit squarely in that category, where quality is expected or mandated but acceptability is desired. We have seen how performance-driven reform would resolve the tension: by pursuing quality and assuming that shortcomings in acceptability result from information problems.

For those on the front lines of reform (public managers), the relationship between what the citizen values and the features of their service performance that they are capable of measuring and maximizing remains elusive. In the absence of information about that relationship, and in the face of new GASB performance reporting standards, the public manager might set about maximizing departmental performance on a set of measures and shaping citizen preferences such that attaining them becomes the definition of service quality. Aware that sharing decision making on service delivery with citizens may have adverse implications for quality, we may expect public managers to become less sensitive to citizen input over service standards, especially if the input conflicts with an established performance standard. The public manager may be reluctant to discontinue formal processes designed to facilitate shared decisions but be even more reluctant to sacrifice quality standards to keep the citizen input process meaningful.

What the reformed public manager really needs is a participatory structure that builds public acceptance without sharing authority for decision making. This is presumed impossible in the citizen participation literature. Moreover, citizens are likely to recognize the participatory structure as a "pseudo-arena," where their input is received but not regarded. If the structures of participation are retained but decision-making authority is not shared, public managers may have to assume a lot more information problems to explain a decrease in citizen satisfaction with service quality and perception of government responsiveness.

Citizens may see the impact of the new commitment to quality in how their services are delivered. Bureaucracy operates on decision rules, and a zone of discretion exists around those rules. Bureaucratic discretion in service delivery takes place in the zone of discretion. The actual service provider, or the "street-level bureaucrat,"[9] is independent from the agency he or she represents and deals with the stress of inadequate resources and vague or contradictory job expectations by developing a set of coping strategies that offer shortcuts to decision making. Identifying a set of performance criteria and defining those criteria as the agency's mission should permit a shortcut to decision making. A service provider (for example, a police officer) should emphasize activities for which performance data are collected and minimize his or her attention to activities not included in the performance criteria. That prospect does not rest easy with many public managers, for obvious reasons. It also does not please finance officials, who expect to confront a situation where resources are secure for activities that are measured and tenuous for activities that are not.

A Political Theory

Twenty years after Key's lament over the lack of a budgetary theory, another political scientist offered an eloquent response. Aaron Wildavsky said, in essence, that any theory that allocates funds to A rather than B is a political theory and not a budgetary theory.[10] In a democracy, decisions about what government should do and how they should be funded are products of a political process, not a decision rule. His words are especially relevant here because the new performance-driven reforms could amount to a political theory, especially if they become part of the financial auditing process. Measuring performance is a value-defining exercise. Whoever sets the performance standards—government officials or the GASB—will imprint their values on the process and change outcomes. Because the philosophy that underpins this reform movement assumes that accountability to citizens can be achieved by a means other than a political process, we may see some remarkable changes in how service bureaucracies operate, how resources are allocated to service areas, and even in how citizen preferences affect service delivery.

The proponents of performance-based accountability are certainly well intentioned, and they may even be right. Emphasis on improving performance seems appropriate when applied to government services and the individuals who deliver them. This cautionary essay simply asks whether we in the public sector may have compromised responsiveness to citizens in our zeal to be more accountable to them—whether we have unknowingly embraced a political theory that tells us whether we should fund activity A or activity B. Perhaps the GASB standards, if implemented, will professionalize service bureaucracies and restore public confidence in government. But we must acknowledge that the reform agenda and the reform rhetoric are not consistent unless we assume that performance goals reflect citizen preferences. As practiced, we assume that performance values are what citizens *should* prefer. If these attitudes become institutionalized through GASB and other professional organizations of public managers, governments will have been presented with a way to demonstrate accountability to their citizens while being less responsive to their preferences.

Notes

1. Key, V. O., Jr. "The Lack of a Budgetary Theory." *American Political Science Review,* 1940, *34,* 1137–1144.

2. Governmental Accounting Standards Board. "Concepts Statement No. 2 of the Governmental Accounting Standards Board on Concepts Related to Service Efforts and Accomplishments Reporting." Norwalk, Conn.: GASB, 1994, paragraph 31.

3. GASB (1994), paragraph 34.

4. See Rivenbark, W. C. "The GASB's Initiative to Require SEA Reporting." *Public Administration Quarterly,* forthcoming.

5. See Brown, R. E., and Pyers, J. B. "Service Efforts and Accomplishments Reporting: Has Its Time Really Come?" *Public Budgeting and Finance,* 1998, *18*(4), 101–113.

6. Government Finance Officers Association. "Service Efforts and Accomplishments Reporting." GFOA policy statement, adopted June 23, 1993.

7. Government Finance Officers Association. "Performance Measurement and the Governmental Accounting Standards Board." GFOA policy statement, adopted Feb. 15, 2002.

8. See Cleveland, H. "How Do You Get Everybody in on the Act and Still Get Some Action?"

Public Management, 1975, *57,* 3–6; Cupps, D. S. "Emerging Problems of Citizen Participation." *Public Administration Review,* 1977, *37,* 478–487; Nelkin, D. "Science and Technology Policy and the Democratic Process." In J. C. Peterson (ed.), *Citizen Participation in Science Policy.* New York: Wiley, 1984; and especially Thomas, J. C. *Public Participation in Public Decisions: New Skills and Strategies for Public Managers.* San Francisco: Jossey-Bass, 1995.

9. Lipsky, M. *Street Level Bureaucracy.* New York: Russell Sage Foundation, 1980.

10. Wildavsky, A. "Political Implications of Budgetary Reform." *Public Administration Review,* 1961, *21,* 183–190.

Janet M. Kelly is associate professor in the Department of Political Science at the University of Tennessee.

Wireless Youth:
Rejuvenating the Net

Anthony G. Wilhelm

It is practically impossible to imagine a future that is not immersed in increasingly portable and minuscule information and communications devices. The new kid on the block in the 1990s, the Internet is rapidly fading into the white noise of our daily experience in this country. This is particularly true for the younger generation, born since 1982, which Neil Howe and William Strauss refer to as Millennials.

According to these authors of *Millennials Rising,* this cohort bears little resemblance to Generation X. Millennials are more numerous, more affluent, better educated, and more ethnically diverse. On the basis of surveys, they describe themselves as optimistic and upbeat about the world in which they are growing up. They are not selfish, like the Me Generation, but are team players. Importantly, they believe in the future, are engaged in civil society, and conceive of themselves as on the leading edge of progress, particularly when it comes to their excitement about and mastery of new technologies.

The potential of this group to improve society and revitalize our democracy using the Internet is confronted by the dominance of entertainment values and rapid consolidation in the media and telecommunications industries. Entertainment values, for example, are eclipsing the educational and civic dimensions of online activity. It is critical that this can-do generation participate in reinventing the medium to improve people's lives, particularly in an increasingly global context. Although the Internet is becoming second nature for many young people, new forms of online civic practice need to ferment and expand to fulfill its full potential as an empowering medium.

The Future Is Here—and It's for Sale

Millennials use many types of technology, instant-messaging friends while doing homework, talking on the phone, and listening to music, all at the same time. Many teenagers have their own Website—their own digital soapbox—and are generally more adept users of technology than their parents. On a typical day, Millennials spend about six and a half hours using media:

watching television, listening to music, reading and working on the computer, and meeting new e-pals, often halfway around the world.[1] What we know, as the great media theorist Marshall McLuhan suggested two generations ago, is that in general people use new media to supplement, not replace, older media. For now, teenagers who spend a lot of time with computers also watch more TV and read more than most others.

Within this media environment, digital technologies and online activities are increasingly occupying youth's attention. E-mail, instant messaging, and chat groups are incredibly popular among teens, as are downloading music files and buying products online. Among eighteen- and nineteen-year-olds, 91 percent use e-mail and 83 percent use instant messaging, with more than half (56 percent) of older teens saying they prefer the Internet to the telephone.[2] With the acceleration of high-speed Internet connections over cable and next-generation wireless tools, where young people are able to color-coordinate and personalize their communications devices, these numbers (and the time youths spend online) will in all likelihood increase.

This digital landscape is not altogether rosy, since many new applications and gizmos under development are geared toward amusement rather than education and engagement. Commercials for high-speed Internet service and faster microprocessors tout the entertainment value of these advances. In Intel ads, for example, sepia-toned aliens learn to use the Pentium 4 processor to play more lifelike video games and to download multimedia entertainment. High-speed broadband services are being marketed as a delivery mechanism for movies-on-demand and interactive video games. Who will deliver health care online or expand distance education opportunities?

The video game industry is just one example of how entertainment values are outstripping demand for noncommercial content. In 2000, sales of hardware and software for interactive games eclipsed Hollywood for the first time, with sales totaling $8.2 billion, compared to $7.75 billion in U.S. movie box-office receipts.[3] There are thousands of titles, many of which are quite violent. Despite the enormous market, and the relatively high penetration of video-gaming consoles (Microsoft's Xbox and Sony's Playstation) in underserved communities, hardly anyone is creating marketable educational content, let alone applications for youths to plug into what's going on in their neighborhoods. As these consoles become more sophisticated and allow young people to connect with gaming partners online, it is critical to develop educational and civic content (such as variations on the popular SimCity), or online experience will become just another diversion for our children. Parents and educators must demand this content, and government must create public venture funds to experiment with socially beneficial applications.

Entertainment applications may be what drive the market, but public and private (philanthropic) funders of technology and media content should devote substantial resources to public media—that is, enterprises that develop the noncommercial, democratic components of digital media. Additionally, public media partnerships, such as those between broadcasting stations and community groups, must focus on fostering diverse voices at the local level; this means underserved young people become an important target to develop their ability to express their aspirations through new media. Even though young adults are the age group least likely to vote, their enthusiasm for new technologies might be just the lever to encourage more young adults to exercise their franchise.

The Markle Foundation in New York City is among the few private philanthropies investing in socially beneficial interactive applications aimed at children. But the scope of the investments is too small to affect the marketplace noticeably. What is needed is substantial public funding for public media content and robust leadership to make the case that these investments are worthwhile. These dollars have to build the capacity of a community to be a producer of its own content, and not just a passive consumer of prepackaged fare. A credible proposal is circulating in Congress to use the proceeds from spectrum auctions to fund these programs.

One example of a program that brings community groups together with media producers to enhance engagement in the larger community is the Benton Foundation's Sound Partners for Community Health (www.soundpartners.org), a partnership with the Robert Wood Johnson Foundation. The program fosters creative solutions to health care problems by linking community organizations with public radio stations to produce programming that addresses local needs. Sound Partners supports sixty-eight partnerships in the United States to demonstrate the civic role that broadcaster and community organization alike can play in the local community. The program amplifies the voices of underserved communities, as illustrated by a partnership between KUAC-FM and Native American youth in Fairbanks, Alaska, in which youths are trained with digital media to undertake a dialogue with listeners about substance abuse and recovery.

Replicating this program through other platforms, such as satellite radio or Webcasting, would lower the cost and expand the scope of what's possible within a budding partnership. Young people are ready-made to get involved in these civic activities and partnerships, because they are invited to connect with their community on their own terms—by using media about which they are already excited—and on issues of relevance to their everyday lives.

A Generation, Divided

If a community is to play a leading role in working with media partners to produce programming and content of value, the digital literacy skills of community members, particularly young people, must be more fully developed. The term *digital literacy* captures the type of capacity that must be cultivated so that a community can effectively use computer applications, video, and Internet tools to improve people's lives. Perhaps the highest order of digital literacy is for the citizen to be a media producer, not just a passive consumer, to use available outlets to voice hopes and concerns. For this to happen, widespread access to digital media is critical, as well as training and mentoring to cultivate young people's talents. Notwithstanding the fact that many youths are Internet-savvy, a significant digital divide still exists in access and training. This disparity is particularly acute in high-poverty and rural communities. Moreover, the retrenchment in national leadership in combating this problem signals a decline in funding and resources to develop locally driven content fully.

Two mega media companies, AOL Time Warner and Bertelsmann, convened a conference in Berlin in March 2002 on twenty-first century literacy. Notables such as German Chancellor Gerhard Schröder and Madeleine Albright, the secretary of state in the Clinton administration, spoke of the power and promise of information and communications technologies to knock down walls (quite an appropriate metaphor given the city's recent history). Schröder boldly asserted that digital literacy should now take its place as a basic literacy alongside reading, writing, and arithmetic, recognizing the pivotal role of information and communications technologies in underwriting life-long learning, economic productivity, and democratic engagement. Given Europe's aging population, policy leaders there recognize the need to enhance productivity among younger workers to sustain the quality of life to which Europeans are accustomed.

Enthusiasm about the advantages of an online society and an interlinked world has persisted through the bursting of the dot com bubble and the events of September 11. The twenty-first-century literacy conference was hosted under the shadow of the Brandenburg Gate. At the time of the conference, the edifice was shrouded under a drop cloth, undergoing restoration and renewal. Since Deutsche Telekom (the AT&T of Germany) is supporting the renovation project, the company took the opportunity to use the gate as a giant advertisement for their Internet service, called T-Online. The slogan brandished across the famous landmark declares that *Im Internet ist alles möglich*: everything is possible with the Internet.

This excitement should be directed toward overcoming the persistent disparities in access within the United States and Europe and between developed and developing nations.[4] Juxtaposed to the reality of poverty and underdevelopment in technology infrastructure, the Deutsche Telekom banner is ironic, symbolizing not only the hopes but also the unfulfilled potential that remains untapped and that requires collective action if it is to be realized.

With more than one billion people in the world between the ages of fifteen and twenty-four, improving livelihood and creating jobs are central challenges, ones that smart use of information and communications technologies may help turn into "digital opportunities." The challenges are immense, given that 80 percent of the world's population has yet to make a phone call and a majority of young people live in developing countries where there is often little opportunity for productive work. To tear down the walls of economic exclusion, we must create markets to raise the standard of living in communities outside the bounds of global trade, or poverty will continue to sow the seeds of animosity and envy between haves and have-nots. The Education Development Center in Boston has teamed with the World Bank to work with youth from five developing countries to initiate business plans for renewable energy enterprises, creating employment opportunity while also tackling environmental degradation. These efforts should be multiplied and supported by investments both in youth leadership and in strengthening the organizational capacity of youth-serving institutions.

In the United States, social exclusion and alienation persists, whether in south Boston or in the tribal lands of the western United States, as communities continue to languish without basic information and communications infrastructure. The high dropout rate and lack of preparedness for employment in today's economy deepen social exclusion. At the end of 2001, only about 14 percent of children living in low-income families were using the Internet at home, compared with 63 percent of children in families earning more than $75,000 per year.[5] With respect to race and ethnicity, as Figure 1 reveals, 50 percent of non-Hispanic white kids used the Internet at home in 2001 compared to only 25 percent of African American children and 20 percent of Hispanics. Many underserved youths also attend public school with little access to and effective integration of emerging technologies, a missed opportunity given what we know about the positive impact of the virtual learning environment in improving the motivation and performance of at-risk

Figure 1. Home Computer and Internet Use Among Children

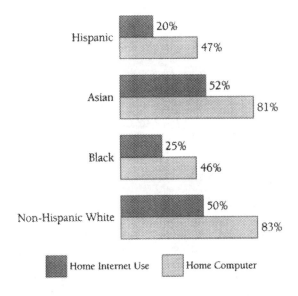

teenagers. Minority-serving institutions, such as tribal colleges and historically black colleges, can only dream of doing what America's elite colleges and universities have accomplished, given the gap in resources.

Although the federal government and leading private sector companies have spent billions of dollars in recent years to improve access to and effective use of computers and the Internet in schools and libraries, there are signs that this commitment is slowing in the wake of economic insecurity and a change of priorities at the top levels of government. Companies that invested heavily in educational technology initiatives, such as AT&T and Lucent, are pulling the plug or scaling back. The federal government is also scuttling programs aimed at building technology capacity in communities, training teachers, and demonstrating technology applications, such as e-government and telemedicine, in underserved communities.

So as the science fiction writer William Gibson declares, the future is here; it's just not equally distributed. Without access to these tools, as well as the ability to use them effectively, we are missing a necessary link in jump-starting and sustaining global educational, economic, and civic advancement aimed at the nearly one billion teenagers and young adults in the developed and developing worlds.

Youths as Producers

Millennials see themselves on the cutting edge of something new. A society and culture in which communications tools are pervasive is second nature for many young adults. Indeed, they themselves are actors and co-creators in its unfolding, as consumers and as producers of new content and applications, the very essence of twenty-first-century digital literacy. Although ownership of many forms of digital information and communications technologies is being consolidated in the hands of a few media conglomerates, the media landscape overall remains far from bleak.

On the one hand, youths and young adults are increasingly the target of corporate advertising campaigns. America's thirty-two million teens accounted for a total of $172 billion in spending in 2001 (half of this cohort is now shopping online).[6] ABC Network's attempt to roundhouse "Nightline" and replace it with David Letterman's "Late Show" to attract advertisers salivating over the young adult niche market underscores this reality.

But on the other hand, in the choices they make as consumers young people can have a potentially significant degree of economic and political influence. In the 1980s, *institutions* used their clout to push for social and political change, as for example in the campaign against apartheid in South Africa. Today *individuals* are exercising their power as consumers (in green-oriented market niches) and investors (favoring socially responsible investments) to influence economic activity. A Marymount University poll of one thousand adults revealed that 75 percent of consumers would avoid shopping at stores that sell clothes made in sweatshops. But of course it is critical to gather and disseminate this kind of information for the cumulative effect of consumer decisions to have an impact. By lowering search costs and making information more widely available, the Internet and other digital technologies can play a strong role in furthering this activity.

Most important, though, youths are not just consumers but producers as well, riding the crest of the wave of new innovation and practice that has blossomed since the middle to late 1990s. Because they have facility with these tools, they have the potential to shape the emerging media landscape for social good.

The power of the Internet and other digital media resides in interactivity, the ability of the user to be a producer and not just a passive recipient, as is the case with one-way, broadcast media. The Internet is also an efficient and effective organizing tool, enabling communities of interest across the globe to broaden the scope of their involvement and engagement at a relatively low transaction cost. Finally, the startup costs in becoming an Internet publisher are sufficiently low to allow a young person in a basement or community center to hurdle entry barriers and potentially reach a global audience.

The young entrepreneur Omar Wasow, who, directly upon graduating from Stanford University, founded New York Online, a cybercommunity of New Yorkers from all walks of life, is now the architect of BlackPlanet (www.blackplanet.com), a Web portal that brings the worldwide African diaspora together into an online community allowing members to cultivate personal and professional relationships, gain access to relevant goods and services, and stay informed about and engaged in the larger world.

On a larger scale, Intel has created the Intel Computer Clubhouse, a model that uses technology to enable inner-city youths to acquire the tools, problem-solving skills, and confidence necessary for a successful life. In partnership with the Museum of Science in Boston, the museum's award-winning Computer Clubhouse, and the MIT Media Lab, Intel is supporting establishment of one hundred Intel Computer Clubhouses in low-income communities worldwide. The Clubhouse is exporting a model of how youths can interact with technology and their society through active engagement, a learning philosophy imbedded in the constructivist theories of Seymour Papert.

On a smaller scale and an ad hoc basis, the exciting mix of youthful enthusiasm for creating and designing coupled with the possibilities inherent in the technologies has generated exciting partnership at the grassroots level across the United States and globally. An initiative in Chicago called Street-Level Youth Media works with inner-city youths in media arts and emerging technologies for use in self-expression, communications, and social change. In developing forms of expression and journalism with new media from the point of view of young people and their concerns, Street-Level Youth Media is a platform for the larger community to hear from youths in their own voice rather than through the lens of mainstream media and its often negative depictions of youth. In sharp contrast to these messages, what is often revealed through youth media is an abiding concern for neighborhood, identity, and global justice. For example, in 1998 Street-Level students visited Chiapas, Mexico, and worked with indigenous youths to train them in video production to present their own view of their plight to an international audience. This use of interactive media to overcome traditional borders of geography and identity arguably reveals a desire for political engagement.

Unlike the diffusion of prior communications tools, adoption and use of new communications and information media is being driven in part by teenagers and young adults. The role of young people in the advent of the printing press in the fifteenth century or the telegraph in the nineteenth century was peripheral at best. The commercial Internet is only fifteen hundred days old; there is great potential for young people to lead as early adopters and shapers of this medium.

Youth Identity in an Era of Globalization

Surveys show that many Millennials are engaged in community service and active in causes such as the effort to improve the environment, potentially reflecting an interest in the unfolding global civil society. In Australia, the struggle of the Mirrar clan against establishment of new uranium mining within their territory has been joined by scores of Australian youths who embrace the justice of their cause. With the Internet, young people can seize the opportunity to reach out and extend their own sense of global identity and responsibility as they reinvent community building for the twenty-first century.

No example better highlights this commitment than the protests surrounding World Trade Organization (WTO) talks, in particular the meetings in Seattle in 1999. At the event, ministers and industrialists convened to discuss the best arrangements to buttress world free trade while, unbeknownst to them, student, labor, and nonprofit groups were using the Internet to organize to counteract this trend.

The emerging internationalism already percolating among Millennials can be furthered by information technology. Electronic conferencing and transorganizational content development hold great potential for cross-cultural dialogue and cooperation among teenagers and young adults. Expanded use of these technologies may transform attitudes by allowing younger generations to compare their respective national values and cultures and lead to better mutual knowledge and understanding.

Rejuvenating the Net

We know that youths care deeply about their community and about social justice, and if they are so motivated then they may rejuvenate the forms of civic practice prevalent on the Web today. As the poet Emily Brontë wrote while a young adult, the aspirations of youth can often be obscured:

Sweet love of youth, forgive, if I forget thee,
While the world's tide is bearing me along;
Other desires and other hopes beset me,
Hopes which obscure, but cannot do thee wrong![7]

The possibilities offered by new technology may channel the desires and hopes of youth into exciting new practice. However, on the basis of my observations and study of Internet conversation as outlined in my book *Democracy in the Digital Age,* I see several trends emerging that may obstruct realization of these promising forms of online cross-cultural dialogue and forums for democratic problem solving.

The first challenge centers on providing information versus seeking information. Particularly when it comes to political chat, participants are more than eager to chime in and express their point of view but substantially less likely to make a request to fill a gap or seek exploration of an alternative view on an issue about which they are interested. Self-expression is clearly important, but youths have to "listen" to each other and to decision makers, entering into dialogue to broach understanding and act collectively in the light of day. In New York City, HarlemLive, a youth Internet publication, recently provided a platform on its Website for young Palestinian refugees to speak about their daily life under occupation.

Second, there is a tendency with information and communications technologies, and the straw polls and plebiscite-like activity rampant on commercial portals, to want to register individual preferences and then aggregate them, rather than encouraging exchange and thoughtful response to discussion threads. We should move away from aggregating preferences and look toward fostering common ground, as well as illuminating and reconciling points of contention that require continuing discussion, debate, and elaboration.

Finally, through chat groups and online discussion forums, participants tend to gravitate toward like-minded individuals so that cyberspace largely becomes an extension of the social networks and hobby groups one would join and belong to in a physical community. What does this homogeneity imply for overcoming difference, encouraging tolerance and understanding, and broadening our horizons, particularly given the global possibilities of these technologies?

Of course the architecture of a network or online discussion, including its functionality, along with the presence of expert moderation, affects the quality of online exchange, and new software ought to be reviewed and tested to increase the quality of online discussion.

Clearly there are many technological hurdles, and technology continues to change so rapidly that it is sometimes hard to keep pace with the latest devices or tools. But these are only tools. The great challenge on the horizon in the twenty-first century is social, not technological: we must come to better terms with our diversity. Encouraging diverse viewpoints and cultures ought to be the hallmark of a liberal society; let us hope the technological innovations and digitally mediated social practices brokered by young people will bring us closer to an inclusive global civil society that honors diversity as its linchpin.

Notes

1. Roberts, D. F., and others. *Kids and Media @ the New Millennium.* Menlo Park: Henry J. Kaiser Family Foundation, 1999.

2. Pastore, M. "Demographics: Internet Key to Communication Among Youth." *Cyberatlas,* Jan. 2, 2002. (http://cyberatlas.internet.com/big_picture/demographics/article/0,,5901_961881,00.html)

3. Kharif, O. "Let the Games Begin—Online." *BusinessWeek,* Dec. 13, 2001. (www.businessweek.com/technology/content/dec2001/tc20011213_2329.htm)

4. For more information on the digital divide, visit the Benton Foundation's Digital Divide Network at www.DigitalDivideNetwork.org. If you are interested in international digital divide issues, please connect with www.DigitalOpportunity.org.

5. Wilhelm, A., Carmen, D., and Reynolds, M. *Connecting Kids to Technology: Challenges and Opportunities.* Baltimore: Annie E. Casey Foundation, 2002.

6. Wood, M. "Teens Spent $172 Billion in 2001." *Teenage Research Unlimited,* Jan. 25, 2002. (www.teenresearch.com/PRview.cfm?edit_id=116)

7. Brontë, E. "Remembrance." (Extract.) In *Emily Brontë: Selected Poems.* New York: St. Martin's Press, 1994, p. 12.

Anthony G. Wilhelm is vice president for programs at the Benton Foundation.

ORDERING INFORMATION

MAIL ORDERS TO:
  Jossey-Bass
  989 Market Street
  San Francisco, CA 94103-1741

PHONE subscription or single-copy orders toll-free to (888) 378-2537 or to (415) 433-1767 (toll call).

FAX orders toll-free to (800) 481-2665.

SUBSCRIPTIONS cost $60.00 for individuals in the U.S./Canada/Mexico and $84 in the rest of the world; $115.00 for U.S. institutions, agencies, and libraries; $155.00 for institutions in Canada and Mexico; and $189.00 for institutions in the rest of the world. Standing orders are accepted. (For subscriptions outside the United States, orders must be prepaid in U.S. dollars by check drawn on a U.S. bank or charged to VISA, MasterCard, American Express, or Discover.)

SINGLE COPIES cost $25.00 plus shipping (see below) when payment accompanies order. Please include appropriate sales tax. Canadian residents, add GST and any local taxes. Billed orders will be charged shipping and handling. No billed shipments to Post Office boxes. (Orders from outside the United States must be prepaid in U.S. dollars drawn on a U.S. bank or charged to VISA, MasterCard, or American Express.)

Prices are subject to change without notice.

SHIPPING (single copies only):	Surface	Domestic	Canadian
	First item	$5.00	$6.00
	Each add'l item	$3.00	$1.50

For next-day, second-day, and international delivery rates, call the number provided above.

ALL ORDERS must include either the name of an individual or an official purchase order number. Please submit your orders as follows:
  Subscriptions: specify issue (for example, NCR 86:1) you would like subscription to begin with.
  Single copies: specify volume and issue number. Available from Volume 86 onward. For earlier issues, see below.

MICROFILM available from University Microfilms, 300 North Zeeb Road, Ann Arbor, MI 48106. Back issues through Volume 85 and bound volumes available from William S. Hein & Co., 1285 Main Street, Buffalo, NY 14209. Full text available in the electronic versions of the Social Sciences Index, H. W. Wilson Co., 950 University Avenue, Bronx, NY 10452, and in CD-ROM from EBSCO Publishing, 83 Pine Street, P.O. Box 2250, Peabody, MA 01960. The full text of individual articles is available via fax modem through Uncover Company, 3801 East Florida Avenue, Suite 200, Denver, CO 80210. For bulk reprints (50 or more), contact Craig Woods at (201) 748-6645 or cwoods@wiley.com.

DISCOUNTS FOR QUANTITY ORDERS are available. For information, please write to Jossey-Bass, 989 Market Street, San Francisco, CA 94103-1741.

LIBRARIANS are encouraged to write to Jossey-Bass for a free sample issue.

VISIT THE JOSSEY-BASS HOME PAGE on the World Wide Web at http://www.josseybass.com for an order form or information about other titles of interest.

NATIONAL CIVIC LEAGUE OFFICERS AND DIRECTORS

2001 Officers
Chair, Dorothy Ridings, Council on Foundations, Washington, D.C.
Vice Chairman, David Vidal, The Conference Board, New York
Treasurer, James D. Howard, Century Pacific, Phoenix, Arizona
Secretary, Carrie Thornhill, D.C. Agenda, Washington, D.C.
President, Christopher T. Gates, Denver
Assistant Treasurer, John W. Amberg, Denver

Board of Directors
D. David Altman, The Murray and Agnes Seasongood Good Government
    Foundation, Cincinnati, Ohio
John Claypool, Greater Philadelphia First, Philadelphia
Patricia Edwards, National Center for Community Education, Flint, Michigan
Badi G. Foster, Tufts University, Medford, Massachusetts
Dr. J. Eugene Grigsby III, University of California, Los Angeles
Hubert Guest, Cheverly, Maryland
Dr. John Stuart Hall, Arizona State University, Phoenix
Dr. Lenneal J. Henderson Jr., University of Baltimore, Baltimore, Maryland
Dr. Theodore Hershberg, University of Pennsylvania, Philadelphia
Curtis Johnson, The CitiStates Group, St. Paul, Minnesota
Anna Faith Jones, Boston Foundation, Boston
Dr. David Mathews, Kettering Foundation, Dayton, Ohio
Robert H. Muller, J.P. Morgan Securities, New York
Sylvester Murray, Cleveland State University, Cleveland
Betty Jane Narver, University of Washington, Seattle
Frank J. Quevedo, Southern California Edison, Rosemead, California
Robert Rawson Jr., Jones, Day, Reavis & Pogue, Cleveland
Juan Sepulveda, The Common Enterprise, San Antonio, Texas
Arturo Vargas, NALEO Educational Fund, Los Angeles
Linda Wong, Community Development Technologies Center, Los Angeles

Honorary Life Directors and Former Chairmen
Terrell Blodgett, Austin, Texas
Hon. Bill Bradley, Newark, New Jersey
Hon. Henry Cisneros, Los Angeles
Hon. R. Scott Fosler, Washington, D.C.
Hon. John W. Gardner, Stanford, California
James L. Hetland Jr., Minneapolis, Minnesota
Hon. George Latimer, St. Paul, Minnesota
Hon. William W. Scranton, Scranton, Pennsylvania
Hon. William F. Winter, Jackson, Mississippi

National Civic League Publications List

ALL PRICES include shipping and handling (for orders outside the United States, please add $15 for shipping). National Civic League members receive a 10 percent discount. Bulk rates are available. See end of this list for ordering information.

Most Frequently Requested Publications

The Civic Index: A New Approach to Improving Community Life
National Civic League staff, 1993
50 pp., 7 × 10 paper, $7.00

The Community Visioning and Strategic Planning Handbook
National Civic League staff, 1995
53 pp., $23.00

Governance

National Report on Local Campaign Finance Reform
New Politics Program staff, 1998
96 pp., $15.00

Communities and the Voting Rights Act
National Civic League staff, 1996
118 pp., 8.5 × 11 paper, $12.00

Forms of Local Government
National Civic League staff, 1993
15 pp., 5.5 × 8.5 pamphlet, $3.00

Guide for Charter Commissions (Fifth Edition)
National Civic League staff, 1991
46 pp., 6 × 9 paper, $10.00

Handbook for Council Members in Council-Manager Cities (Fifth Edition)
National Civic League staff, 1992
38 pp., 6 × 9 paper, $12.00

Measuring City Hall Performance: Finally, A How-To Guide
Charles K. Bens, 1991
127 pp., 8.5 × 11 monograph, $15.00

Model County Charter (Revised Edition)
National Civic League staff, 1990
53 pp., 5.5 × 8.5 paper, $10.00

Modern Counties: Professional Management—The Non-Charter Route
National Civic League staff, 1993
54 pp., paper, $8.00

Term Limitations for Local Officials: A Citizen's Guide to Constructive Dialogue
Laurie Hirschfeld Zeller, 1992
24 pp., 5.5 × 8.5 pamphlet, $3.00

Using Performance Measurement in Local Government: A Guide to Improving Decisions, Performance, and Accountability
Paul D. Epstein, 1988
225 pp., 6 × 9 paper, $5.00

Model City Charter (Seventh Edition)
National Civic League staff, 1997
110 pp., 5.5 × 8.5 monograph, $14.00

Alliance for National Renewal

ANR Community Resource Manual
National Civic League Staff, 1996
80 pp., 8.5 × 11, $6.00

Taking Action: Building Communities That Strengthen Families
Special section in *Governing Magazine,* 1998
8 pp., 8.5 × 11 (color), $3.00

Communities That Strengthen Families
Insert in *Governing Magazine,* 1997
8 pp., 8.5 × 11 reprint, $3.00

Connecting Government and Neighborhoods
Insert in *Governing Magazine,* 1996
8 pp., 8.5 × 11 reprint, $3.00

The Culture of Renewal
Richard Louv, 1996
45 pp., $8.00

The Kitchen Table
Quarterly newsletter of Alliance for National Renewal, 1999
8 pp., annual subscription (4 issues) $12.00, free to ANR Partners

The Landscape of Civic Renewal
Civic renewal projects and studies from around the country, 1999
185 pp., $12.00

National Renewal
John W. Gardner, 1995
27 pp., 7 × 10, $7.00

San Francisco Civic Scan
Richard Louv, 1996
100 pp., $6.00

1998 Guide to the Alliance for National Renewal
National Civic League staff, 1998
50 pp., 4 × 9, $5.00

Springfield, Missouri: A Nice Community Wrestles with How to Become a Good Community
Alliance for National Renewal staff, 1996
13 pp., $7.00

Toward a Paradigm of Community-Making
Allan Wallis, 1996
60 pp., $12.00

The We Decade: Rebirth on Community
Dallas Morning News, 1995
39 pp., 8.5 × 14 reprint, $3.00

99 Things You Can Do for Your Community in 1999
poster (folded), $6.00

Healthy Communities

Healthy Communities Handbook
National Civic League staff, 1993
162 pp., 8.5 × 11 monograph, $22.00

All-America City Awards

All-America City Yearbook (1991, 1992, 1993, 1994, 1995, 1996, 1997)
National Civic League staff
60 pp., 7 × 10 paper, $4.00 shipping and handling

All-America City Awards Audio Tape Briefing
Audiotape, $4.00 shipping and handling

Diversity and Regionalism

Governance and Diversity:
Findings from Oakland, 1995
Findings from Fresno, 1995
Findings from Los Angeles, 1994
National Civic League staff
7 × 10 paper, $5.00 each

Networks, Trust and Values
Allan D. Wallis, 1994
51 pp., 7 × 10 paper, $7.00

Inventing Regionalism
Allan D. Wallis, 1995
75 pp., 8.5 × 11 monograph, $19.00

Leadership, Collaboration, and Community Building

Citistates: How Urban America Can Prosper in a Competitive World
Neal Peirce, Curtis Johnson, and John Stuart Hall, 1993
359 pp., 6.5 × 9.5, $25.00

Collaborative Leadership
David D. Chrislip and Carl E. Larson, 1994
192 pp., 6 × 9.5, $20.00

Good City and the Good Life
Daniel Kemmis, 1995
226 pp., 6 × 8.5, $23.00

On Leadership
　John W. Gardner, 1990
　220 pp., 6 × 9.5, $28.00

Politics for People: Finding a Responsible Public Voice
　David Mathews, 1994
　229 pp., 6 × 9.5, $20.00

Public Journalism and Public Life
　David "Buzz" Merritt, 1994
　129 pp., 6 × 9, $30.00

Resolving Municipal Disputes
　David Stiebel, 1992
　2 audiotapes and book, $15.00

Time Present, Time Past
　Bill Bradley, former chairman of the National Civic League, 1996
　450 pp., paper, $13.00

Transforming Politics
　David D. Chrislip, 1995
　12 pp., 7 × 10, $3.00

Revolution of the Heart
　Bill Shore, 1996
　167 pp., 8.5 × 5.75, $8.00

The Web of Life
　Richard Louv, 1996
　258 pp., 7.5 × 5.5, $15.00

Programs for Community Problem Solving

Systems Reform and Local Government: Improving Outcomes for Children, Families, and Neighborhoods
　1998, 47 pp., $12.00

Building Community: Exploring the Role of Social Capital and Local Government
　1998, 31 pp., $12.00

The Transformative Power of Governance: Strengthening Community Capacity to Improve Outcomes for Children, Families, and Neighborhoods
　1998, 33 pp., $12.00

Building the Collaborative Community
　Jointly published by the National Civic League and the National Institute for Dispute Resolution, 1994
　33 pp., $12.00

Negotiated Approaches to Environmental Decision Making in Communities: An Exploration of Lessons Learned
　Jointly published by the National Institute for Dispute Resolution and the Coalition to Improve Management in State and Local Government, 1996
　58 pp., $14.00

Community Problem Solving Case Summaries, Volume III
    1992, 52 pp., $19.00

Facing Racial and Cultural Conflicts: Tools for Rebuilding Community (Second Edition)
    1994, $24.00

Collaborative Transportation Planning Guidelines for Implementing ISTEA and the CAAA
    1993, 87 pp., $14.00

Collaborative Planning Video
    Produced by the American Planning Association, 1995
    6-hr. video and 46 pp. workshop materials, $103.00

Pulling Together: A Land Use and Development Consensus Building Manual
    A joint publication of PCPS and the Urban Land Institute, 1994
    145 pp., $34.00

Solving Community Problems by Consensus
    1990, 20 pp., $14.00

Involving Citizens in Community Decision Making: A Guidebook
    1992, 30 pp., $30.00

NATIONAL CIVIC LEAGUE sales policies: Orders must be paid in advance by check, VISA, or MasterCard. We are unable to process exchanges, returns, credits, or refunds. For orders outside the United States, add $15 for shipping.

TO PLACE AN ORDER:

CALL the National Civic League at (303) 571–4343 or (800) 223–6004, or

MAIL ORDERS TO:
    National Civic League
    1445 Market Street, Suite 300
    Denver, CO 80202–1717, or

E-MAIL the National Civic League at ncl@ncl.org

United States Postal Service

Statement of Ownership, Management, and Circulation

1. Publication Title	2. Publication Number	3. Filing Date
National Civic Review	0 0 2 7 . 9 0 1 3	9/26/02

4. Issue Frequency	5. Number of Issues Published Annually	6. Annual Subscription Price
Quarterly	4	$60.00 Individual $115.00 Institutio

7. Complete Mailing Address of Known Office of Publication (Not printer) (Street, city, county, state, and ZIP+4)	Contact Person
989 Market Street San Francisco, CA 94103-1741 San Francisco County	Joe Schuman
	Telephone
	415 782 3232

8. Complete Mailing Address of Headquarters or General Business Office of Publisher (Not printer)

Same as above

9. Full Names and Complete Mailing Addresses of Publisher, Editor, and Managing Editor (Do not leave blank)

Publisher (Name and complete mailing address)

Jossey-Bass, A Wiley Company
Above Address

Editor (Name and complete mailing address)
Robert Loper
National Civic League
1319 F Street NW, STE 204
Washington, DC 20004

Managing Editor (Name and complete mailing address)

None

10. Owner (Do not leave blank. If the publication is owned by a corporation, give the name and address of the corporation immediately followed by the names and addresses of all stockholders owning or holding 1 percent or more of the total amount of stock. If not owned by a corporation, give the names and addresses of the individual owners. If owned by a partnership or other unincorporated firm, give its name and address as well as those of each individual owner. If the publication is published by a nonprofit organization, give its name and address.)

Full Name	Complete Mailing Address
John Wiley & Sons Inc.	111 River Street Hoboken, NJ 07030

11. Known Bondholders, Mortgagees, and Other Security Holders Owning or Holding 1 Percent or More of Total Amount of Bonds, Mortgages, or Other Securities. If none, check box ➔ ☐ None

Full Name	Complete Mailing Address
Same as Above	Same As Above

12. Tax Status (For completion by nonprofit organizations authorized to mail at nonprofit rates) (Check one)
The purpose, function, and nonprofit status of this organization and the exempt status for federal income tax purposes:
☐ Has Not Changed During Preceding 12 Months
☐ Has Changed During Preceding 12 Months (Publisher must submit explanation of change with this statement)

PS Form 3526, October 1999   (See Instructions on Reverse)

13. Publication Title	14. Issue Date for Circulation Data Below
National Civic Review	Summer 2002

15. Extent and Nature of Circulation			Average No. Copies Each Issue During Preceding 12 Months	No. Copies of Single Issue Published Nearest to Filing Date
a.	Total Number of Copies (Net press run)		2,284	1,997
b. Paid and/or Requested Circulation	(1)	Paid/Requested Outside-County Mail Subscriptions Stated on Form 3541. (Include advertiser's proof and exchange copies)	680	642
	(2)	Paid In-County Subscriptions Stated on Form 3541 (Include advertiser's proof and exchange copies)	0	0
	(3)	Sales Through Dealers and Carriers, Street Vendors, Counter Sales, and Other Non-USPS Paid Distribution	701	699
	(4)	Other Classes Mailed Through the USPS	0	0
c.	Total Paid and/or Requested Circulation [Sum of 15b. (1), (2),(3),and (4)] ▶		1,381	1,341
d. Free Distribution by Mail (Samples, complimentary, and other free)	(1)	Outside-County as Stated on Form 3541	0	0
	(2)	In-County as Stated on Form 3541	0	0
	(3)	Other Classes Mailed Through the USPS	1	1
e.	Free Distribution Outside the Mail (Carriers or other means)		281	319
f.	Total Free Distribution (Sum of 15d. and 15e.) ▶		282	320
g.	Total Distribution (Sum of 15c. and 15f) ▶		1,663	1,661
h.	Copies not Distributed		621	336
i.	Total (Sum of 15g. and h.) ▶		2,284	1,997
j.	Percent Paid and/or Requested Circulation (15c. divided by 15g. times 100)		83%	81%

16. Publication of Statement of Ownership
☐ Publication required. Will be printed in the __Winter 2002__ issue of this publication. ☐ Publication not required.

17. Signature and Title of Editor, Publisher, Business Manager, or Owner   Susan E. Lewis | Date

Susan E. Lewis   VP & Publisher - Periodicals   9/26/02

I certify that all information furnished on this form is true and complete. I understand that anyone who furnishes false or misleading information on this form or who omits material or information requested on the form may be subject to criminal sanctions (including fines and imprisonment) and/or civil sanctions (including civil penalties).

Instructions to Publishers

1. Complete and file one copy of this form with your postmaster annually on or before October 1. Keep a copy of the completed form for your records.

2. In cases where the stockholder or security holder is a trustee, include in items 10 and 11 the name of the person or corporation for whom the trustee is acting. Also include the names and addresses of individuals who are stockholders who own or hold 1 percent or more of the total amount of bonds, mortgages, or other securities of the publishing corporation. In item 11, if none, check the box. Use blank sheets if more space is required.

3. Be sure to furnish all circulation information called for in item 15. Free circulation must be shown in items 15d, e, and f.

4. Item 15h., Copies not Distributed, must include (1) newsstand copies originally stated on Form 3541, and returned to the publisher, (2) estimated returns from news agents, and (3), copies for office use, leftovers, spoiled, and all other copies not distributed.

5. If the publication had Periodicals authorization as a general or requester publication, this Statement of Ownership, Management, and Circulation must be published; it must be printed in any issue in October or, if the publication is not published during October, the first issue printed after October.

6. In item 16, indicate the date of the issue in which this Statement of Ownership will be published.

7. Item 17 must be signed.

Failure to file or publish a statement of ownership may lead to suspension of Periodicals authorization.

PS Form 3526, October 1999 (Reverse)